Yvonne Morris is currently Children's Adviser for the Diocese of Oxford, helping, supporting, training and advising churches and their workers on their ministry with children. Yvonne still gets to practise ministry locally at St Matthew's and Luke's Churches in Oxford, where she was Youth and Children's Minister for ten years before taking up her diocesan role and, further afield, working with tweens on summer camps for West Runton Holidays. Yvonne's husband, Anthony, and their son and daughter keep her very rooted. Yvonne is author of Side by Side with God in Everyday Life *(Barnabas for Children, 2011).*

CW01095161

Barnabas
for
Children®

Barnabas for Children® is a registered word mark and the logo is a registered device mark of The Bible Reading Fellowship.

Text copyright © Yvonne Morris 2014
The author asserts the moral right
to be identified as the author of this work

Published by
The Bible Reading Fellowship
15 The Chambers, Vineyard
Abingdon OX14 3FE
United Kingdom
Tel: +44 (0)1865 319700
Email: enquiries@brf.org.uk
Website: www.brf.org.uk
BRF is a Registered Charity

ISBN 978 0 85746 021 9
First published 2014
10 9 8 7 6 5 4 3 2 1 0

Acknowledgements
Unless otherwise stated, scripture quotations are taken from the Contemporary English Version of the Bible published by HarperCollins Publishers, copyright © 1991, 1992, 1995 American Bible Society.

Scripture quotations taken from The Holy Bible, New International Version® (Anglicised edition) copyright © 1973, 1978, 1984, 2011 by www.biblica.com, Biblica, Inc.® Used by permission of Hodder & Stoughton Publishers, an Hachette UK company. All rights reserved. 'NIV' is a registered trade mark of Biblica. UK trademark number 1448790.

Scripture quotations from The New Revised Standard Version of the Bible, Anglicised edition, copyright © 1989, 1995 by the Division of Christian Education of the National Council of the Churches of Christ in the United States of America. Used by permission. All rights reserved.

Cover photo: Dad and son © monkeybusinessimages/iStock/Thinkstock; Mum and daughter © Jupiterimages/Stockbyte/Thinkstock

A catalogue record for this book is available from the British Library

Printed by Gutenberg Press, Tarxien, Malta

Exploring God's Love

in Everyday Life

Readings to help children grow in their faith

Yvonne Morris

This book is dedicated to the memory of my dear father-in-law Mick Morris, who died on 15 May 2013. His life so gently, generously and humorously displayed his love of Jesus and Jesus' love of him as they meandered quietly together side by side, day by day.

— ☀ —

Acknowledgements

I'd like to say a specific thank you to the McKemey family, whose questions about God's love and 'Love your enemies' started this whole project, and to Steve and Jenny Hellyer, who continue to support and guide me with care, wisdom and wit. Thanks to Marguerite Hutchinson and Olivia Warburton, who have kept the project on track and on time for BRF. Finally, to my Mum and Dad, who have built such firm, loving foundations for our family, and to Ant, Tash and Josh as we continue to journey with God and each other.

Love is patient, love is kind.
It does not envy, it does not boast, it is not proud.
It is not rude, it is not self-seeking,
it is not easily angered, it keeps no record of wrongs.
Love does not delight in evil but rejoices with the truth.
It always protects, always trusts,
always hopes, always perseveres.
Love never fails.

1 CORINTHIANS 13:4–8 (NIV 1984)

Contents

※

Foreword

Love. It sounds so simple, and yet there is nothing more foundational for children to understand than what true love really looks like. In a world that tries to warp love into myriad self-serving definitions, God's essence glows with the healthy, life-giving truth of his love. Our children were designed to be loved by God and us, and to love God and others in return. But if you are like me, between getting your children clean and moving them to where they need to be on time, you will often feel that you are missing something in helping them really grasp the fullness of God's love.

What Yvonne Morris offers us as parents in her superb book is a chance to delve into scripture with our children, understand more of God's love and wonder together about what it means for us today in our complex lives. Each chapter takes us gently through a different aspect of God's love. Together with our children, we look at God's love through the prism of Bible stories and sharing our experiences of life. Yvonne doesn't let us shy away from the difficult bits of life but guides us to face the realities of love in a broken world and helps us wonder together about being loved by God and loving others in the face of our imperfections. God's love is real and powerful, and this book takes us on a family journey of knowing and living this truth more and more.

Exploring God's Love in Everyday Life brilliantly encourages us not just to talk about God's love but also to encounter it. Each chapter draws us to connect with God face-to-face and heart-to-heart, so that the truth of what we learn gives us and our children a springboard into personal time with him.

As a parent and Family Life pastor, I am so excited by this book. I want my son to know in every part of his being what it means to be fully loved by God, and I want him to love God with all he has in him. I want him to overflow with God's love and compassion and to serve and love others whole-heartedly all his life. I want every family I serve to be equipped to make God's love something they can explore together with confidence and passion. I am so grateful to Yvonne for writing this book as a tool for all of us to understand more and more 'how wide, long, high and deep' is God's love.

Rachel Turner (author, speaker, and children's and youth work trainer)

Introduction

Love is talked about a lot in our world. Love is everywhere! People are in love, adverts use love to sell products, people sing about love and researchers research love. People talk about God's love and, in the words of one famous song, 'love is all around'.

Sometimes 'love' can seem to be quite selfish or dependent upon how we look or the things we wear or own. Yet God's great love is not like that. God shows us a far wider, longer, higher and deeper love in the things Jesus said and did. God's love is both tough and easy at the same time, and the New Testament shows us everything we need to know, in order to understand this tough love and what it means for the way we live as followers of Jesus.

Exploring God's Love in Everyday Life helps children and grown-ups alike—and together—to discover the length and breadth of this love as Paul set it out in his list of what love is and isn't, does and does not do, in 1 Corinthians 13:4–8. It also puts this list alongside some of the things Jesus said and commanded about love.

As we explore what it means to be disciples of Jesus in this way, my prayer takes the form of Ephesians 3:16–19:

> *I pray that out of his glorious riches he may strengthen you with power through his Spirit in your inner being, so that Christ may dwell in your hearts through faith. And I pray that you, being rooted and established in love, may have power, together with all the Lord's holy people, to grasp how wide and long and high and deep is the love of Christ, and to know this love that surpasses knowledge—that you may be filled to the measure of all the fullness of God.*

EPHESIANS 3:16–19 (NIV)

How to use this book

Find a regular time when you can be together to read, talk, wonder and pray together through the themes and ideas in the book. Don't feel you have to answer all the questions that will be asked. Not knowing answers is fine. Be honest and work out together how you might find out what you need to know.

The chapters take their overall structure from the wording in Ephesians 3:18—'how wide and long and high and deep'—plus a final thought in the 'Love tough' section.

How wide
This section tells a Bible story that presents the general concepts of the theme.

How long
Next comes a second Bible story that brings in a different angle or another way of looking at the concept.

How high
This section offers wondering-type questions or thoughts to stimulate discussion on the theme. Don't be tied to them, though, if you or the children have other questions or subjects you'd like to talk about. When you use wondering questions, allow plenty of time and space to consider them. I've had children come back to me days after a wondering time to tell me where they've got to in their thinking. If wondering seems hard at first, persevere. Don't be afraid of silence: assume that the child is processing internally. Sometimes children can't find the words to express what they're thinking or feeling, so find other ways to help them to express themselves—for example, in pictures, symbols, song, making or art.

When you are invited to 'talk together', do just that. The 'How high' section isn't a lecture to be given; it provides talking points to start conversation and discussion. Be released and relaxed to go where the child leads.

How deep

'How deep' aims to nurture a two-way relationship with God. The key elements are:

- Decide what you want to say to God about the theme.
- Tell God what you'd like to say. Ask him what you need to ask. Be quiet and listen to what God wants to say to you.

Take time to engage with the 'How deep' section. Our aim is to connect with God and to be open to God connecting with us and our children. Asking God questions and waiting for him to answer can teach us how God speaks to us—sometimes directly with words or pictures, dreams or thoughts, and sometimes indirectly through other people or other stories.

In this section, you and the children are encouraged to pray in your own words. You can't go wrong here. Remember that God doesn't need fancy words or even any words at all. In learning to go deeper with God, you are learning and practising communication with him. This can take time, and it seems easier at some times than others. Stick with it. These are exactly the tools the children will need on a lifelong journey with God.

Most of all, my prayer is that you discover and hear God in new ways and that you and the children will grow as disciples, secure in his love for you and willing to step out in faith and share with others the outrageous grace that is the love of Christ.

Love tough

As we know, the world demonstrates and demands ways of being that are not always the ways of God. This final section gives an opportunity to think through what it means for each of us to live out God's love and to consider what impact that has on the choices we make as we seek to follow Jesus side by side, day by day.

Please note: this isn't meant to induce guilt and a sense of failure when we get things wrong (the world does enough of that). Rather, by opening the themes, stories and possibilities of God at work in our lives, it enables us more easily to see God at work and recognise when we are growing in his ways. My hope is that the ways of exploring, wondering and praying together that are encouraged in this book will form parts of a tool kit that equips the disciple (of whatever age) for the lifelong journey of faith.

Love is patient

'Love is patient' is a difficult starting point when we don't feel patient. Other people can annoy us in the way they do things. Sometimes we don't want to wait or we feel frustrated because we can't translate an idea into action. Yet Jesus showed amazing patience throughout his life and that reveals a lot about how God loves you and me.

Right at the beginning of Jesus' life, there was a man who knew that God had promised to send his Messiah, his Chosen One, to help people be reunited with God. He had waited patiently for his prayers to be answered and, at long last, he saw God's answer in a tiny human baby.

How wide

Simeon was an old man who lived in Jerusalem. He loved God and tried hard to live the right way for God. Simeon talked with God often and he was waiting for the writings of old to come true and for his prayers to be answered.

One day he felt God's Spirit with him very strongly. Simeon heard God's voice say, 'Simeon, my son, you will see the one I have sent. My Messiah will be known to you before I bring you home to me for ever.'

'Where will I see him, Lord?' Simeon replied.

Knowing that he was sensing God's Spirit again, Simeon went out into the temple court just as a family with a tiny week-old baby were coming out. The family had brought birds to sacrifice to say 'thank you' to God, as the religious custom said they should.

Simeon went over and, in love, gazed at the child. 'May I take him?'

he asked the father. As the parents looked at each other, not quite sure what was happening, the old man took the baby into his arms. 'Oh Lord,' he gasped, 'thank you.' Then he continued his prayer.

'God, my King. You promised I would see your Messiah before I died. Thank you that I have seen him. My heart is at peace because you have answered the prayers of many. Thank you for this child who will rescue your people and be a light in the darkness for everyone. Bless these, his parents, in what you have called them to do.'

Looking up into the baby's mother's eyes, Simeon spoke to her: 'This child is destined to cause the falling and rising of many in Israel. He is a sign for, and from, God. He will reveal what is in people's hearts. Many will hate him for what he shows. It will feel like a sword stabbing your soul too.'

RETOLD FROM LUKE 2:25–35

How long

When Jesus was a grown man, he spent a lot of time travelling around, telling people stories (often called 'parables') to help them know God and his ways. This is one of his stories.

The kingdom of heaven is like a king who wanted to sort out his affairs and get back money that some of his servants owed him. The first servant came before the king knowing that he owed a *lot* of money.

'You owe me 10,000 talents,' said the king. 'I want it back.'

'But, your majesty, I need more time to get the money. I don't have it right now.'

'Well, I've waited long enough. You'll have to raise the money by selling everything you own. Your wife and children should make good slaves and raise quite a bit of cash.'

Throwing himself to the floor, the servant pleaded, 'Your majesty,

I beg you, I promise I'll pay you back. Just give me more time. Please don't make me sell my family.'

The king was filled with pity and compassion for his servant. 'All right,' he said, 'I release you from your debt. You owe me nothing.'

Overcome with relief, the servant breathed again. 'Oh, your majesty, thank you, thank you, thank you.'

As the servant went out from the king's presence, he bumped into a fellow servant who happened to owe him 100 denarii. It was quite a lot of money, but not as much as 10,000 talents. Suddenly overcome with anger, he grabbed the man. Half-choking him, he shouted, 'You owe me money! I want it back right now!'

'Please, I need more time,' the man begged, but the first servant refused and had him thrown into prison until he could pay the debt.

Other servants saw what happened and were greatly troubled. They went to the king to tell what they had seen. The king was furious and called the first servant back.

'You wicked man,' he said. 'I cancelled all your debt because you begged me to. Why did you not show mercy to the man who owed you?'

The king had the servant taken to prison until he could pay back his debt.

Jesus said, 'This is how my heavenly Father will treat you unless you forgive others from your heart.'

RETOLD FROM MATTHEW 18:21–35

How high

I wonder when you've had to be very patient.

I remember being pregnant and waiting for the baby to come. That was pretty hard at times because when you are waiting for a baby to come, you feel very big and fat; it's hard to get comfy in bed; you can't bend down easily if your shoes need tying up and it is hard to breathe because the baby is squishing your insides. I remember getting to the point of trying to wait patiently for the time I knew God had for the baby to be born, but wishing it could be sooner.

I find, even now, that waiting sometimes seems easy and other times it seems really hard. Talk together about your experiences of times when you've had to wait patiently for something.

Of course, patience isn't just about waiting for things or events. In our 'How long' story, the king showed great patience with his servant, but the servant didn't extend the same courtesy.

I wonder when you feel least patient and what the consequence of your impatience is. Once, I was struggling with a piece of artwork and got so cross that I screwed it up and threw it across the room in a fit of frustration. I am also aware of the times I shout, 'Hurry up!' to my children and am not very patient. These times are often in the mornings when we are trying to leave the house to go to school and work. But, in all honesty, my impatience never really helps any of us speed up. It only makes us feel more annoyed with each other.

When I feel impatient, it's often because I am thinking about myself and my needs ahead of others'. Having a patient attitude with people, or in tricky situations, or when provoked or under strain, gives us opportunities to demonstrate God's love and patience. Talk together about what you think this might mean or look like.

Do you find it hard to be patient in prayer? It can feel as if God isn't listening to us or answering our prayers—but did you know that, in the Old Testament story of Daniel, there was a time when Daniel was praying and God sent out an angel to give Daniel a reply, but the angel got delayed for three weeks? (Check out the story in Daniel 10.) A wise Christian once told me that when we ask God to give us patience, he will, but he will also give us opportunities and choices to put that patience into practice.

How deep

Psalm 40:1–3 says:

I patiently waited, Lord, for you to hear my prayer.
You listened and pulled me from a lonely pit
full of mud and mire.
You let me stand on a rock with my feet firm,
and you gave me a new song,
a song of praise to you.
Many will see this and they will honour
and trust you, the Lord God.

What do you want to say to God about 'Love is patient'? Tell him what you'd like to say. Ask him what you need to ask. Be quiet and listen to what God wants to say to you.

Love tough

Think about how you behave when you are feeling patient. What are the signs that tell you impatience is rising?

> *Don't forget that the Lord is patient because he wants people*
> *to be saved. This is also what our dear friend Paul said when*
> *he wrote to you with the wisdom that God had given him.*
>
> 2 PETER 3:15

Living in God's ways means that we have to 'love tough' and choose to be different. Talk with God about this and ask him how you can 'love tough' and show his patient love.

✸

Love is kind

The Roman philosopher Seneca once said, 'Wherever there is a human being there is an opportunity for kindness.' 'Love is kind' gives us a chance to explore whether Jesus showed us more than the obvious ways to be kind, in his thoughts as well as in his actions.

How wide

It was getting late. Jesus had healed many people who were in need. It was almost time for the Jewish festival of Passover, and Jesus went up a mountain with his disciples and sat down.

When Jesus saw the large crowd, he asked Philip, 'Where will we get enough food to feed all these people?' Jesus was really testing Philip, since he already had a plan.

Philip answered, 'There are so many people. Don't you know we would need a year's wages to pay for a little bread for them all?'

Andrew spoke up. 'Here is a boy who has five small loaves of barley bread and two fish. But what good is that with all these people?'

'Get everyone sitting down in groups,' Jesus instructed the disciples. There were about five thousand men on the mountainside that day. Jesus took the bread and gave thanks to his Father. Then they passed the bread among the people. He did the same with the fish and everyone there had plenty to eat.

All the people ate all they wanted, and when they were done Jesus told his disciples to gather up the leftovers, so that none would be wasted. The disciples did so, and filled twelve large baskets with what was left from the five small barley loaves.

The people who had witnessed the miracle began to say to each other, 'This must be the Prophet who is to come into the world!' Jesus realised that they would try to force him to be their king, so he went away up on a mountain, where he could be alone.

RETOLD FROM JOHN 6:1–15

How long

Jesus was teaching in the temple in Jerusalem. Among the people gathered there were chief priests and religious leaders.

Jesus said, 'I've got a story to tell you. Then tell me what you think. A father had two sons. He went to the older son and said, "Go and work in the vineyard today." But the son replied, "Not right now. I'm busy." Later on, he was sorry for what he'd said, so he went to the vineyard and helped out.

Meanwhile, the man went to his younger son and said, "Go and work in the vineyard today." "OK, I'll be right there," said the younger son, but he got distracted on the way and didn't go to work. Which one of the sons obeyed his father?'

'The older one,' answered the chief priests.

'You are right,' said Jesus. 'And you can be sure that tax collectors and prostitutes will get into God's kingdom before you ever will. John the Baptist showed you how to get ready and do right, but you would not believe him. These sinners did believe. But even when you realised that they believed, you still would not change your minds and believe.'

RETOLD FROM MATTHEW 21:28–32

How high

Have you ever been told to 'be good'? When I was a young girl visiting my grandma, she would often ask, 'Have you been good?' before giving me a treat or some pocket money. I must confess now to always saying 'Yes' to her, even if I wasn't exactly sure what she meant. I might have done something a bit naughty but I had also done lots of things right or well, or I'd listened to instructions or helped my mum or been a good friend. I hadn't actively been naughty the whole time.

Now, as a parent, I always say to my children, 'Be kind and helpful.' This is much more measurable and it means that when I ask *if* my children have been kind and helpful, I can then ask them *how*. It gives many more opportunities to share the good news stories of the day and hear of acts of kindness offered to friends, classmates and teachers at school.

Do you think there is a difference between being 'good' and being 'kind'? Talk together about this.

Do you think that kindness is only about doing kind things or is there more to it? I wonder if being helpful and thoughtful, not speaking out too quickly, not being wrongly critical, being truthful, noticing the things others are good at and mentioning them and being courteous are also ways of demonstrating kindness. Are there other things that you would add to this list?

Now have another look at the 'How wide' and 'How long' stories. Where do you see kindness in a broader sense in the stories? Jesus said that what we think is as important as what we do. How do the stories show this in action?

Kindness is one of the 'fruit of the Holy Spirit' that Paul talks about in Galatians 5:22, and is one of the ways we can tell if we are growing in God's ways. Acts of kindness, which help others or make them happy, show that we, like our Father God, want to build others up and encourage and love them.

How deep

What do you want to say to God about 'Love is kind'? Tell God what you'd like to say. Ask him what you need to ask. Be quiet and listen to what God wants to say to you.

Luke 1:78 says, 'God's love and kindness will shine upon us like the sun that rises in the sky.' Pray that God's love and kindness will shine upon others through you today.

Love tough

Think about the difference that kindness makes in the world around us and what you see when people are unkind.

> *The Law was given by Moses, but Jesus Christ brought us*
> *undeserved kindness and truth.*
>
> JOHN 1:17

Living in God's ways means that we have to 'love tough' and choose to be different. Talk with God about this and ask him how you can 'love tough' and show his loving kindness even when it seems that others are ungrateful or unkind to us.

Love does not envy

Envy can cause us to feel discontented with what we have or who we are. God's love asks us not to be envious, but to be content instead with what God has given us. So in this chapter we will explore what 'Love does not envy' looks like and see if we can work out how God's tough love helps us to be content.

How wide

There was once a man who had two sons. One day, his younger son came to him and said, 'Father, I want my share of the inheritance now.' So with a heavy heart the father gave his son his share of all the father's wealth.

A short while later, the younger son packed up his belongings and set off for adventures in a foreign country. He had a brilliant time, enjoying amazing parties, buying this and that and splashing his money around so that people hung out with him. But once his money was gone, his 'friends' left him, he couldn't party any more and, as a famine spread through the land, he had no food to eat either. What a mess he'd got into!

Knowing he had to do something, the young man got a job looking after pigs for a local farmer. Oh, how he would have loved to eat some of the pig food! But he had nothing.

Looking after the pigs gave him plenty of time to think about what he'd done, and eventually a thought occurred to him. 'My father's workers have plenty to eat, yet here I am starving to death. What I should do is go home, confess to my father what I've done and ask him to allow me to work as a hired help in his fields. At least then I'll be home and I won't starve.'

Feeling foolish, he trudged home, practising his speech as he went.

As he turned the corner on the final part of his journey home, he saw a man in the distance—someone moving towards him, and moving towards him at great speed.

The father was running to his son. Seeing him from a long way off, he thought his heart would burst. Running to him as fast as he could, he took his son in his arms, hugging and kissing him.

'Father, I have sinned against God and against you and I am not good enough to be your son any more,' said the son, but his father was not paying any attention. Already turning to his servants, he said, 'Go and get him new clothes and new shoes, and a ring for his finger, and prepare a great feast. We must celebrate. My son was dead but has come back to life. He was lost and now is found.'

As the party started in the house, the older son was coming in from his work in the field. Hearing the music, dancing and laughter, he called to the servant, 'What's going on?'

'Your brother is home safe and sound and your father has ordered a celebration,' came the reply.

'WHAT?!' Anger raced through the elder son. How dare his father do this?

His father came out, saying, 'Isn't it wonderful that your brother is home?' But he could see that it was not such wonderful news to his other son.

'For years I've worked so hard for you and been obedient and yet you've never let me have a dinner party for my friends. He's wasted all your money, worried you sick, and now that he's back you give him a massive party! How is that fair?'

'My son, my son,' his father soothed. 'You are always with me, and everything I have is yours. But we must be glad and celebrate, because your brother was dead but has come back to life. He was lost and now is found.'

RETOLD FROM LUKE 15:11–31

Wonder together about how the two sons were envious. Wonder about how love overcame envy in this story.

How long

The Holy Spirit led Jesus into the desert, so that the devil could test him. Jesus hadn't eaten for six whole weeks and was hungry and weak. The devil came to him and said mockingly, 'If you really are God's Son, change these stones into bread and feed your hunger.'

'Scripture says, "Nobody can live only on food,"' Jesus replied. 'People need the words that God has spoken too.'

Next, the devil transported Jesus into the holy city and stood next to him on the highest part of the temple. 'Why don't you jump?' he asked. 'After all, it is promised in the scriptures that "God will instruct his angels to catch you so that your feet won't be hurt on the stones."'

Jesus answered, 'The scriptures also say, "Do not test the Lord your God!"'

Finally, the devil took Jesus up a very high mountain and showed him all the kingdoms on earth and their power. 'All this is yours,' he said. 'I give it to you… if you will only bow down and worship me.'

Summoning all his strength, Jesus answered, 'Go away, Satan! The scriptures say, "Worship the Lord your God and serve only him."'

The devil left Jesus, and angels came to help him.

RETOLD FROM MATTHEW 4:1–11

How high

I wonder if you've ever felt envy. What did it look or feel like to you?

Do you notice that, in our society today, people are encouraged never to be contented with what they have? There is always a better toy, phone or TV, or someone more beautiful, more talented or richer than you. Advertising tries to make us envious of others so that we will go and buy stuff that they say will make us feel better about ourselves. It's a great promise but it never really delivers, because it's all about stuff on the outside, like possessions, clothes or the way we look.

Can you imagine either of the Bible stories in 'How wide' and 'How long' as an advert for God's love on television? What do you think such adverts would show?

The nature of God and the way he loves us mean that he is less concerned with material possessions and outward appearance and more concerned about what is inside us. Proverbs 14:30 says, 'A heart at peace gives life to the body, but envy rots the bones' (NIV). Perhaps one of the reasons for this is that being envious is about 'me' and what I want, and is especially selfish if it leads to a person doing wrong or hurting others in order to get what they want. Maybe God wants us to love others in such a way that we are glad about what they have for themselves and grateful for what we have.

I don't think that God wants us to be without nice things. It's more about how we view and think about what we have or don't have. We are reminded of this in Hebrews 13:5: 'Don't fall in love with money. Be satisfied with what you have. The Lord has promised that he will not leave us or desert us.'

A wise person once said to me that if you see something you think you want, you should consider if you really need it. If you don't really need it, wait until the next day to see if you still want it.

How deep

Spend some time thinking about what makes you envious of your friends, whether it's their possessions or families or personalities (you could write these things down). Then talk with God about how you can be more peaceful and secure in who God has made you to be.

What do you want to say to God about 'Love does not envy'? Tell

God what you'd like to say. Ask him what you need to ask. Be quiet and listen to what God wants to say to you about who you are and how he has made you. Again, it may be helpful to write your thoughts down.

Remember that in our 'How wide' story, the father welcomed his son back and celebrated. Reflect on how this is like God's love for you.

Love tough

Think about how you behave when you are feeling envious. Do you give your parents a hard time, demanding that they get you the thing you want? Do you actively dislike someone because you wish you could sing or dance or do maths like they do?

> *Don't be annoyed by anyone who does wrong, and don't envy them. They will soon disappear like grass without rain. Trust the Lord and live right!*
>
> PSALM 37:1–3

Living in God's ways means that we have to 'love tough' and choose to be different. Talk with God about this and ask him how you can 'love tough' and not be envious.

Love does not boast

Have you ever heard or used the word 'boast'? Even if you haven't, I'm sure you've experienced it! The Oxford English Dictionary defines 'to boast' as 'to talk with excessive pride and self-satisfaction about one's achievements, possessions, or abilities'. My grandad was a fisherman and he told a few 'The fish was *this* big!' stories. I wonder if you have boasted or told a story about something that happened to you, making out that your part in it was much bigger, or the thing was more dramatic than it really was. But 'Love does not boast' is on Paul's list of what love is and isn't, so let's explore what that might mean for us in seeking to live out God's tough love.

How wide

Jesus was talking to a crowd, teaching them about God's ways.

'When you do good things, don't show off about it. If you do, you won't get a reward from your Father in heaven. And when you give to the poor and needy, again, don't show off about it. That's what the loudmouths do in the meeting places and on the street corners, because they are looking for praise. But I can assure you that they already have their reward.

'When you give to the poor, don't tell anyone about it. Make your gift in secret. Your Father God knows what you do in secret and will reward you. In the same way, when you pray, don't be like those show-offs who just love to stand up and pray in the meeting place and on the street corner. They only do it to look good among people. But I assure you, they already have their reward.

'When you pray, go to your room or a private place and be alone with God. Pray to your Father God in private, because he knows what you do in private, and he will reward you. When you pray, don't chatter on and on like the people who don't know God. They think God likes to hear long prayers. But don't be like them. Your Father God knows what you need before you ask. Pray like this:

'Our Father in heaven, help us to honour your name. Come, set up your kingdom so that everyone on earth will obey you, as you are obeyed in heaven. Give us our food for today. Forgive us for doing wrong as we forgive others who wrong us. Keep us from being tempted and protect us from evil.

'If you forgive others when they wrong you, your Father in heaven will forgive you when you do wrong.'

RETOLD FROM MATTHEW 6:1–14

How long

As they journeyed towards Jerusalem, Jesus and his disciples came to the village of Bethphage. They rested for a while, but all too soon their thoughts turned towards the next part of their journey and they talked about the coming Passover festival.

Jesus sent two of the disciples on to the next village with instructions to bring a donkey: 'In the next village, you'll quickly find a donkey with her colt. Untie them both and bring them to me. If anyone asks what you're doing, just say, "The Lord needs them." Then you won't have any problems.'

This part of Jesus' story meant that God's promise from long ago came true. A prophet once said, 'Announce to the people of Jerusalem, "Your king is coming to you! He is humble and rides on a donkey. He comes on the colt of a donkey."'

As the disciples entered the village, they saw the two donkeys, just as Jesus had said. Looking around, they saw no one who seemed to own the animals, but while they were untying them, a man came out. 'What are you doing?' he demanded. The disciples were a little unsure. 'Er,' they said, 'the Lord needs them.'

Just as Jesus had said, this was the password they needed. Without any trouble, they brought the donkey and her colt to Jesus and laid some cloaks on their backs. Then Jesus got on.

Along the road to Jerusalem, many people gathered. They spread their clothes on the road and some laid down branches from the trees. The people surrounded Jesus, walking ahead and behind him, and as they walked, they cheered and shouted, 'Hooray for the Son of David! God bless the one who comes in the name of the Lord! Hooray for God in heaven above!'

People in Jerusalem caught the excitement when Jesus entered the city, but they asked, 'Who can this be?'

'This is Jesus,' the crowd answered. 'This is Jesus, the prophet from Nazareth in Galilee.'

RETOLD FROM MATTHEW 21:1–11

How high

One of my all-time favourite books is *The Wind in the Willows* by Kenneth Grahame. The story revolves around the adventures of the four main characters, Mole, Water Rat, Badger and Toad. Toad is a brilliant character, not least because he is the most boastful and conceited animal you could imagine. He loves to tell tales of his adventures, making himself out to be much braver, much cleverer, more cunning and more adventurous than he really was. Often he makes it sound as if only he was involved, when really his friends were just as important, if not more so.

Have you ever experienced this? Perhaps someone at school has boasted, and you felt that it was unjust because you or other friends played a part in their achievement too. Why do you think people boast? In our 'How wide' story, Jesus said that people shouldn't do or say things just to make themselves look good. How do you feel about this?

In *The Wind in the Willows*, there comes a point in the story when Toad realises how boastful he is. He knows that it is no longer appropriate for him to tell such stories about himself, so in the privacy of his room he sings one last song about himself and then resolves to be a more humble toad. You will need to read *The Wind in the Willows* to see if Toad managed to be more humble or not.

Toad was always thinking of himself, and the Christian thinker and writer C.S. Lewis once said, 'Humility is not thinking less of yourself; it is thinking of yourself less.' What do you think he meant by this? Wonder together about what C.S. Lewis said.

Is there ever a time when boasting is OK? Talk together about the difference between boasting and being rightfully pleased with yourself and your achievements. Think about how you feel when your friends or classmates boast. Do you feel pleased for them or do you get cross if they are making outrageous claims about themselves?

Why do you think Paul included 'Love does not boast' in his list of what love is and isn't? In his letter to the Philippians, Paul said, 'Don't be jealous or proud, but be humble and consider others more important than yourselves' (Philippians 2:3).

Talk together about how our 'How high' and 'How long' stories help or hinder us in our understanding of 'Love does not boast'.

How deep

I wonder if 'Love does not boast' is about feeling secure in who God made us and knowing that God loves us. When we want to make ourselves look better or more important, it is sometimes because we feel a bit insecure, uncertain or even shy. We end up talking about ourselves firstly because we all know about ourselves and secondly so that others will give us attention.

Be aware of how you feel when others are boasting. How might you demonstrate God's love in these situations?

What do you want to say to God about 'Love does not boast'? Tell him what you'd like to say. Ask him what you need to ask. Be quiet and listen to what God wants to say to you.

Psalm 44:8 says, 'We boast about you, our God, and we are always grateful.' Having spent a whole chapter exploring why we shouldn't boast about ourselves, here it seems that we are being encouraged to boast about God. How do you feel about that?

I think it's OK to boast about God and the way he blesses us. God is so generous and merciful and loving and surprising that we should be bursting to share his story. (I know it's not always that easy, of course.) Spend some time talking to God about the idea of boasting about him and see if you can make Psalm 44:8 your prayer for today.

Love tough

Try hard to remember this verse from Philippians 2:3: 'Don't be jealous or proud, but be humble and consider others more important than yourselves.'

Living in God's ways means that we have to 'love tough' and choose to be different. Talk with God about this and ask him how you can 'love tough' and be more aware of his love for you when you are in danger of boasting about anything other than God's great love.

Love is not proud

There is a 'right' kind of pride, when you are deeply pleased or satisfied with something that you or someone you know has done. But there is also the kind of pride which means that a person thinks extraordinarily highly of themselves, so as to make others feel less valued or important. 'Proud' is the second 'love is not' in the list of what love is and isn't. In this chapter we will explore what pride looks like and consider how it gets in the way of our love for others and God.

How wide

Jesus was in Bethany, visiting Simon. While they were eating, a woman came to Jesus. She carried an alabaster jar filled with expensive perfume. She poured the oil on his head, it flowed down and the fragrant aroma filled the air.

'Oi! What are you doing?' shouted the disciples indignantly. 'What a waste of perfume!' 'Interrupting our dinner like this!' 'Think of the money we could have made selling that perfume.' 'We could've given the money to the poor.'

'Friends, friends!' Jesus calmed them. 'Why trouble this woman? She has done a great thing for me. There will always be poor people among you, but you will not always have me. This woman poured perfume on my body to get me ready for burial. I tell you the truth, when people tell stories about me and God's good news, what this woman has done will be included in those stories. She will be remembered.'

RETOLD FROM MATTHEW 26:6–13

How long

Dear brothers and sisters,

I am sure that you are full of love and goodness. I am also sure that you have learnt much about God and his ways and that you are able to teach others. I have written to you because there are some things I want you to remember. I've done this because God has given me a special gift to be able to tell those who aren't Jews about Jesus. I serve God in this way.

I am proud of what I have done for God in Christ Jesus. Through knowing Jesus and with the Holy Spirit in me, I lead people (not just Jews) to obey God. They have obeyed God because of what I have said and done, because of the miracles and great things they've seen and because of the power of the Holy Spirit. I have travelled a long way to tell the story of Jesus to those who have never heard it, and many have come to know him. As it is written in scripture, 'Those who were not told about him will see, and those who have not heard about him will understand.'

RETOLD FROM ROMANS 15:14–21

How high

Many years ago, when I was a teenager, I played hockey for a club in the town I lived in then, Luton in Bedfordshire. At the end of the season there was always a club awards evening when trophies were presented for best players and top scorers (you know the sort of thing). Another player and I had scored most of the goals that year but we hadn't kept proper records, so no one really knew who was top. But when the team captain asked which of us had scored the most, my teammate immediately said, 'Yvonne has scored more than me; she should get the trophy.' She said it in such a way that it wasn't open to negotiation. That was it! She had spoken. To be honest, to this day, I'm not sure I had actually scored more goals, but I got the trophy that year. Her act of humility has stayed with me in my attitude and sportsmanship, and every time I see that trophy I remember her, not the goals I scored.

It's not that my teammate wasn't pleased with her own achievement; she just really didn't mind whether anyone else knew about it or not. I wonder if anything like this has happened to you?

You might have heard the saying 'Pride comes before a fall'. It's based on the writings in the book of Proverbs in the Old Testament part of the Bible. Proverbs 11:2 says, 'When pride comes, then comes disgrace, but with humility comes wisdom' (NIV) and Proverbs 16:18 says, 'Pride goes before destruction, a haughty spirit before a fall' (NIV).

I wonder what this might mean. Do you have any stories of times when you've seen or experienced it?

I wonder if pride is in the list of what love is and isn't because it is seen when you put yourself first and show off your wealth, possessions, cleverness or other abilities by putting others down. If you have spent time looking at 'Love does not boast', I'm sure there is much in 'Love is not proud' that feels familiar. Talk together about what you think are the similarities and differences between pride and boasting.

God wants us to be rightly proud of the gifts he has given us and for us to use them in the right ways, but not at the expense of others. Psalm 10:4 also gives us an insight, because it says, 'In their pride the wicked do not seek him; in all their thoughts there is no room for God' (NIV 1984). If we have no room for God in our thoughts, then we are too full of other things. Do you see this in the 'How high' and 'How long' stories today?

How deep

What do you want to say to God about 'Love is not proud'? Tell God what you'd like to say. Ask him what you need to ask. Be quiet and listen to what God wants to say to you.

Have another look at Psalm 10:4: 'In their pride the wicked do not seek him; in all their thoughts there is no room for God.' Perhaps you could take a moment to say sorry to God if there has been no room for him in your thoughts today.

Many of the psalms in the Old Testament are songs that help people remember and take 'right' pride in all the good things God has done for his people. Here are some verses from the beginning of Psalm 105:1–5:

Praise the Lord and pray in his name!
Tell everyone what he has done.
Sing praises to the Lord!
Tell about his miracles.
Celebrate and worship his holy name with all your heart.
Trust the Lord and his mighty power.
Remember his miracles and all his wonders
and his fair decisions.

Why not have a go at writing your own prayer or song showing a right pride or boasting in God and the part he plays in your life?

Love tough

Living in God's ways mean that we have to 'love tough' and choose to be different. Talk with God about this and ask him how you can 'love tough' and be rightly proud in God for the gifts and talents he has given you, but not at the expense of putting others down or thinking less of them.

Love is not rude

Rudeness brings anger, frustration, hurt, pain and even fear to the world, so it's easy to see why it's on the list of what love is and isn't. The stories today help us to examine what being rude might or might not look like and encourage us to be increasingly mindful of our actions, choices and words.

How wide

In the distance they saw the group. 'Do you think that's him?' they asked each other. Slowly, slowly, the travelling group got nearer to the village, the men waiting, watching, wondering if he was among them. Then one shouted out, 'Jesus, Master, please have pity on us!'

Jesus looked at them and saw them—really saw them as God sees them. 'Go and show yourselves to the priests,' he said.

Was that it? Was that the healing? Were those the words that would enable them to return to their families?

Yes! It was. As the ten men went to find the priest, their scaly skin became whole again. Their leprosy was healed. They could return, the priest confirmed.

One of the healed men, originally from Samaria, ran into the village, searching. 'Where is he?' he asked the astonished villagers. 'Where is Jesus?' Finally he saw Jesus again. Falling at his feet, he praised God. 'Thank you, Master, thank you. I praise God for you and thank you for healing me.'

'Weren't ten of you healed? Where are the other nine?' said Jesus. 'Why was this foreigner the only one to come back to thank God?' Then Jesus told the man, 'Get up and go home. Your faith has made you well.'

RETOLD FROM LUKE 17:11–19

How long

The party was going so well! Jesus was enjoying the company of his friends, the disciples. His mother was also there, enjoying the celebration. That is, Mary was enjoying it until she heard that the wine had run out. She sought out her son.

'They don't have any more wine,' she whispered to Jesus.

'Mother, my time has not yet come. You must not tell me what to do,' he replied. But Mary turned to the servants and said, 'Do whatever Jesus tells you to do.'

There were six enormous stone jars. They each held 20–30 gallons of water, which was used for washing according to religious rules. Jesus told the servants to fill the jars to the brim. It took a while, but when it was done the servants returned to Jesus. 'The jars are full, Master,' they said.

'Now take a cup of the water to the man in charge of the feast,' Jesus instructed.

The servants did so and the man in charge drank the water—which had now been turned into wine. He didn't know where the wine had come from, but the servants did. The man in charge called the bridegroom over and said, 'It is normal at these feasts to give the best wine first. Then, after the guests have enjoyed plenty, other wine is served. But you have kept the best wine until last!' Slightly bemused, the bridegroom returned to his bride as the celebrations went on.

This was Jesus' first miracle. In the village of Cana, Jesus showed his glory and his disciples put their faith in him. Afterwards, he went with his mother, brothers and disciples to the town of Capernaum, where they stayed for a few days.

RETOLD FROM JOHN 2:1–12

How high

This happened when I was at junior school. One lunch time, my friend dared me to ask the dinner lady if I could go to the toilet and, while doing so, call her a rude name. Well, you are not going to believe it, but I took the dare. To this day I don't know why I did, but I remember going up to her, rehearsing the line in my head and wondering how quietly I could slip in the rude name, for the dare to stand. I could have backed out at any moment. I knew I shouldn't do it—but it was a dare.

I mumbled the line and the next thing I knew, she was marching me towards the head teacher's office. I'm sure you can imagine my horror. I had only ever been to the head to show good work, never for being naughty, but now a very cross dinner lady was leading me to the office for a telling off. With a lot of fast talking and apologies, I got a reprieve, but it was close and any punishment would have been thoroughly deserved.

That event happened over 30 years ago, but I can still remember it clearly—the sunshine, the smell of the early summer air, my friend waiting by the climbing frame, watching (clearly not believing I was actually going through with it), and the slight feeling of sickness that I had deliberately been rude to an adult.

Talk together about your experiences of being deliberately rude. What is it like when someone is rude to you?

Being rude to people may not just be about the things we do or don't say; it can involve our tone of voice, gestures or actions. For example, turning your back on someone can be rude, or even being late for an appointment. In the Bible, Titus helps us with this when he says, 'They must always be ready to do something helpful and not say cruel things or argue. They should be gentle and kind to everyone' (Titus 3:1–2). Back in the Old Testament, in Leviticus, it says, 'Stand up in the presence of the aged, show respect for the elderly and revere your God. I am the Lord' (Leviticus 19:32, NIV).

Talk together about our 'How wide' and 'How long' stories. Do you think the nine lepers were being rude by not saying 'thank you' to Jesus, or were they just so delighted that they rushed straight back to their families? (Perhaps it was a bit like when you get a great birthday present and start playing with it straight away. It's not that you're not grateful; you're just so pleased that you simply must play with it.)

Thinking about the 'How long' story, wonder together if Jesus' mother was being rude by speaking out against his wishes and if Jesus was being rude to his mum with his reply.

How do these stories help or hinder our understanding of 'Love is not rude'?

How deep

What do you want to say to God about 'Love is not rude'? Include saying sorry for times when you know you've been rude and saying 'thank you' to God for something he has done for you.

Tell him what you'd like to say. Ask him what you need to ask. Be quiet and listen to what God wants to say to you.

Psalm 51:10 says, 'Create pure thoughts in me and make me faithful again.' Can you make this your prayer for today?

Love tough

In one of the letters he sent, the apostle Peter wrote:

> Do you really love life? Do you want to be happy? Then stop saying cruel things and stop telling lies. Give up your evil ways and do right, as you find and follow the road that leads to peace. The Lord watches over everyone who obeys him, and he listens to their prayers.

1 PETER 3:10–12

Living in God's ways means that we have to 'love tough' and choose to be different. Talk with God about this and ask him how you can 'love tough' by choosing words and actions that bring light, rather than darkness, to others.

*

Love is not self-seeking

In our culture, where it seems as if a lot of people want to be famous celebrities, the concept 'Love is not self-seeking' goes against the norm. It can be really hard to keep serving others when we get little, or no, thanks or praise. So in this chapter we will explore how we can become more secure in God's love for us, knowing that he sees what we do even when no one else does.

How wide

It was the evening of the Passover festival. Jesus knew the time had come when he would leave this world and return to his Father. He loved his followers in this world; he loved them to the very end. Before the evening meal had even started, the devil had persuaded Judas Iscariot to betray Jesus, but Jesus knew that he had come from God and that he would return to God. He also knew that God had given him complete power.

During the meal, Jesus got up, took off his outer garment and wrapped a towel around his waist. The disciples watched him, wondering what he was doing as he picked up a jar of water and poured the water into a bowl.

He knelt down at Andrew's feet, washing them and then drying them with the towel. Then he moved to Jude, then Thomas, then Judas, then Philip, then Matthew, washing and drying their feet. Simon Peter was next, but he moved his feet away, saying, 'Lord, are you really going to wash my feet?'

'You don't really know what I'm doing now, but later you will understand,' Jesus answered.

'You will never wash my feet!' Peter replied.

'If I don't wash you, then you don't really belong to me,' Jesus told him.

Peter wasn't sure about this answer, so he said, 'Well then, Lord, don't just wash my feet. Wash my hands and my head too.'

Jesus answered, 'People who have bathed and are clean all over need to wash just their feet. And you, my disciples, are clean, except for one of you.'

The disciples looked at one another. 'What does he mean?' they were thinking, but Jesus knew who would betray him. After Jesus had finished washing all their feet, he put his outer garment back on and sat down again.

RETOLD FROM JOHN 13:1–12

How long

A heated debate was going on between the disciples as they walked along the road. Walking a little behind, Jesus wondered what they were talking about but he didn't interrupt. When they got home to Capernaum, Jesus asked them, 'What were you all arguing about along the way?' Embarrassed that he had noticed, none of them really wanted to confess that their argument had been about which one of them was the greatest. Now that he was asking them about it, it seemed very silly, so they each looked down and didn't want to answer.

Jesus sat down and gathered the twelve disciples around him. He said, 'If you want the place of honour, you must become a slave and serve others!'

Jesus saw a child walking past the door and called her to him. He put his arm around her to reassure her and spoke again to the disciples. 'When you welcome even a child because of me, you welcome me. And when you welcome me, you welcome the one who sent me.'

RETOLD FROM MARK 9:33–37

How high

Talk together about what you imagine the disciples said to each other in their argument about who was the greatest. Have you ever had an argument like this with your friends?

If you had been a disciple at the table, would you have let Jesus wash your feet?

Television presenter Oprah Winfrey once said, 'Lots of people want to ride with you in the limo, but what you want is someone who will take the bus with you when the limo breaks down.' Would you take the bus or would you only go for the ride in the limo? Who is the person who would accompany you on the bus? If this is a metaphor for life, how is God's love shown through riding in the limo and riding on the bus?

Sometimes it is hard to keep doing things for others, especially when they don't notice, because it can make you feel as if they don't value you. I wonder if you have ever felt like this or if you have realised when people such as your parents, carers or teachers feel like this. It's hard for us as humans to keep serving others without any kind of thanks or recognition. Even though we know we shouldn't need it, we can't help wanting it.

There could be a couple of challenges in this today. One is to notice the things that other people do for you that you don't normally notice and perhaps show them some gratitude. It will probably be easy to spot your packed lunch or clean uniform, but what about the school cleaner who ensures you don't sit on a muddy carpet, or the caretaker who unlocked the doors and gates for you to get into school, or your football coach who turns up to training week after week?

The second challenge is to do something nice for someone in secret. It could be to think of something that you normally get nagged about, like picking up the laundry, tidying your room or helping to lay the table. It could be making a card to cheer someone up, helping someone in need at school or inviting a new person to join your game. But remember, it's to show God's love to others, not so that someone says, 'Well done' to you.

How deep

What do you want to say to God about 'Love is not self-seeking'? Tell him what you'd like to say. Ask him what you need to ask. Be quiet and listen to what God wants to say to you.

Psalm 40:5 says, 'You, Lord God, have done many wonderful things, and you have planned marvellous things for us. No one is like you! I would never be able to tell all you have done.'

Spend some time praising God for the marvellous things he has done for you. How many different things can you see, smell, feel, taste and hear that speak to you of God's great goodness?

Love tough

Living in God's ways means that we have to 'love tough' and choose to be different. Talk with God about this and ask him how you can 'love tough' and not seek thanks or praise for the kind, helpful and loving things you do, but enjoy the joy that others feel.

Love is not easily angered

'Love is not easily angered' is not the same as 'love does not get angry'. Being slow to anger enables greater self-control but sometimes, as our stories today demonstrate, getting angry can challenge or change an unjust or sinful situation.

How wide

Jesus went into the temple and chased out everyone who was buying and selling. He threw over the tables of the moneychangers and the benches of the dove sellers. 'Scripture says, "My house should be called a place of worship." But you have turned it into a place where robbers hide!' he told them.

Blind and lame people came to Jesus in the temple, and he healed them all. Children were praising God and worshipping Jesus. The chief priests and the religious leaders were angry when they saw his miracles and heard the children. 'Do you hear what they're saying?' they asked Jesus.

'Yes, of course,' Jesus answered. 'Don't you know that the scriptures say, "Children and infants will sing praises"?'

Jesus taught in the temple until the evening, when he and the disciples went back to the village of Bethany to spend the night. The chief priests and religious leaders were angry at what Jesus had said, so they started to look for a way to kill him. But they were afraid of Jesus because the crowds loved his teaching.

RETOLD FROM MATTHEW 21:12–19

How long

The disciples had forgotten to bring bread with them on to the boat and now they realised they only had one loaf between them and they were all hungry. 'Watch out!' Jesus told them. 'Guard against the yeast of the Pharisees and of Herod.'

'What's he on about now?' one disciple whispered. 'What on earth does he mean?' said another. 'Perhaps he's just saying it because we don't have any bread,' said another.

Jesus knew what they were thinking and asked them, 'Why are you talking about not having any bread? Don't you understand? Are your minds still closed? Are your eyes blind and your ears deaf? Don't you remember how many baskets of leftovers you picked up when I fed those 5000 people with only five small loaves of bread?'

'Of course we remember. There were twelve baskets,' the disciples answered, slightly bemused.

'And how many baskets of leftovers did you pick up when I broke seven small loaves for 4000 people?'

'Seven baskets,' they answered.

'Don't you know what I am talking about by now?' Jesus asked.

RETOLD FROM MARK 8:14–21

Unlike the apostles, of course, we know that Jesus was telling his followers not to worry about small things, like what they were going to have for lunch, and to watch out for the more important dangers, like the Pharisees and Herod. Jesus knew that God would take care of all their needs, but his followers hadn't learned to trust God quite that much yet.

How high

In our 'How wide' story today, Jesus was clearly angry. In his anger he threw over the money tables and drove the merchants and moneychangers out of the temple. Jesus was justly angry. His anger was directed in a specific way because he was cross and probably sad that his Father's house, which should have been a place of prayer and refuge for sinners in need, had become a place where sin was openly taking place. Theft, fraud and fear were the sins of the temple merchants, under the disguise of helping people carry out the rituals that God required. In a way, it seems that they were sinning in God's name. This is an oxymoron. (If you're not sure, an oxymoron is a phrase in which two words or concepts are put together that contradict each other. For example, 'speed up slowly' or 'sin in God's name'.)

I wonder if you think Jesus was right to behave the way he did in the temple. What else might he have done to show his displeasure?

Do you think Jesus is getting frustrated with the disciples in the 'How long' passage? It seems to me that Jesus was slow to get angry with his disciples, even though, in many of the stories, they just don't seem to get what he is talking about.

What happens when you get angry? I remember one time when my son was about three years old. I had got cross and shouted at him and he said, 'When you shout you look like a monster.' I think I probably felt like a monster too! Talk together about your experiences of being angry or being on the receiving end of someone's anger.

One of the worst aspects of being angry is that we can lose control of ourselves, saying and doing things that can hurt others or ourselves or damage objects. I think this is why 'Love is not easily angered' is on the list of what love is and isn't. It's not that we won't feel angry. In fact, feeling angry at injustice or wrongdoing can sometimes cause us, like Jesus, to take action that leads to a better world for everyone.

How deep

'Love is not easily angered' is really hard to remember, especially when you feel you are not being listened to or are not getting what you want. Did you know that in Proverbs 14:29 it says, 'It's clever to be patient, but it's stupid to lose your temper'?

What do you want to say to God about 'Love is not easily angered'? Tell him what you'd like to say. Ask him what you need to ask. Be quiet and listen to what God wants to say to you.

Write a prayer or poem about how it feels to be angry or on the receiving end of anger.

Love tough

Proverbs 15:18 says, 'Losing your temper causes a lot of trouble, but staying calm settles arguments.'

Living in God's ways means that we have to 'love tough' and choose to be different. Talk with God about this and ask him how you can 'love tough' by staying calm to settle an argument, being slow to anger, or using anger at an unjust situation to make a change for good.

Love keeps no record of wrong

Have you ever heard the phrase 'let bygones be bygones'? It's a very old phrase originating from the late 1300s, which means 'let what has gone before go; forget past disagreements and be reconciled'. It seems that through all ages and times, people have struggled to 'let bygones be bygones' and in this chapter we'll explore what the Bible says about it, using Paul's words, 'Love keeps no record of wrong'.

How wide

When Jesus returned to Capernaum, the people in the town heard that he had come home. They gathered to hear him tell stories and teach, but so many came that the house was completely full. People sat and stood where they could, inside and outside, as close as possible to Jesus to hear his words. As Jesus was speaking, some men came to the house. They were carrying their friend who was paralysed and couldn't move himself. They could see the crowd from the street.

'We'll never get him there,' one said.

'The crowd is too big,' said another.

'What shall we do? We've got this far, we can't give up now.'

'Look,' said the fourth, pointing to the steps. 'The roof—come on!'

It took a lot of effort but they got their friend on to the roof. Then they started chipping away, bashing and digging, making a hole. It took a little while and the people below wondered what was going on, but finally they lowered the man down, right in front of Jesus.

When Jesus saw the faith of the four friends, he said to the paralysed man, 'Son, your sins are forgiven.'

Now some of the religious teachers were there. They heard Jesus' words and couldn't help thinking to themselves, 'Why does he talk like that? He's blaspheming! Only God can forgive sins.'

Immediately Jesus knew in his spirit what they were thinking in their hearts. 'Why are you thinking these things?' he challenged them. 'Which is easier to say: "Your sins are forgiven" or "Get up and walk"? Well, I want you to know that the Son of Man has authority on earth to forgive sins.' Then he turned to the man and said, 'Get up and walk.'

There, in front of everyone, the man got up, picked up his mat and walked home. Everyone was amazed! They had never seen anything like it. In their amazement, the man's friends could only praise God.

RETOLD FROM MARK 2:1–12

How long

Two criminals were led out to be put to death with Jesus. When the soldiers came to the place called 'Skull Hill', they nailed Jesus and the criminals to their crosses and hoisted them up. Jesus was in the middle, with the criminals on each side.

'Forgive them, Father. They don't know what they're doing,' Jesus prayed.

A crowd was watching the crucifixions, and the soldiers played games for Jesus' clothes. People in the crowd mocked Jesus, shouting out, 'He saved others. Why doesn't he save himself?' and, 'If he's really God's chosen Messiah, he'll get himself down from there.'

The soldiers made fun of Jesus too: 'If you are the king of the Jews, save yourself!' They made a sign that said, 'This is the King of the Jews' and hung it over his head.

Even one of the criminals next to him also insulted him: 'Aren't you the Messiah? Save yourself and save us!' But the other criminal told him off: 'Don't you fear God? Aren't you getting the same punishment as this man? We got what we deserve, but him, he did no wrong.' Then he said to Jesus, 'Remember me when you come into your kingdom!'

Jesus answered him, 'I promise that today you will be with me in paradise.'

RETOLD FROM LUKE 23:32–43

How high

Are there any stories in your family about great squabbles or fallings out?

I had a great-uncle who, according to family legend, held a grudge against his brother for years because the brother never paid back the 'five bob' (five shillings) he'd borrowed. Can you imagine having a lifelong quarrel over the equivalent of 25p? It seems incredible, but my great-uncle felt he had been wronged—perhaps even lied to, if promises of return had been made and broken. Having read the 'How wide' and 'How long' stories, what do you think Jesus would want to say to my great-uncle?

In our 'How wide' story, Jesus asks a great question. 'Which is easier to say, "Your sins are forgiven" or "Get up and walk"?' Talk about this together. Which do you think is easier for God and why?

Have you ever imagined what it would look like if God did keep a list of all the wrong things you had said, done or thought, or the good things you had not done? In my case, I can't imagine how long a list that would be! Thankfully, though, whenever we say sorry to God and repent, in his mercy and love the list is gone, erased—there is no record. That is why we can say a prayer called the 'confession' in church every week or even every day. Praying a 'sorry' prayer helps us to become aware of our shortcomings and talk with God about them, then to be made clean from our sins.

I wonder, though, if there is ever a time when it is right to 'keep a record of wrongs'. I was once talking to another mum who wanted to let her son go to a nearby shop unaccompanied, but the journey involved crossing a road. She told me that his track record on obedience and using the Green Cross Code of stopping, looking and listening at the roadside wasn't brilliant, so she didn't know if she could trust him to go out on his own. She was worried that he wouldn't cross the road safely. Do you think she was right to remember in this case, or is this example unhelpful? Talk about it together and share any other stories from your own experiences.

Another example when it is definitely right to keep a record is if you are being bullied. If you have talked to your parents or teachers about it, they may have told you to write down a list of things that happen. You should continue to do so until it is all sorted out. They ask you to do this so that justice can be done and the bully is made accountable for their actions. When the time comes and the situation is dealt with, you can get rid of the list, physically by handing it over, but also emotionally and spiritually, because you don't need to hold on to those events any more.

How deep

God spoke to the prophet Isaiah and gave him a message to share with God's children, the Israelites.

God begins by reminding the Israelites of exactly who he is and the nature of his relationship with them:

> My people, you are my witnesses and my chosen servant.
> I want you to know me, to trust me, and understand that
> I alone am God. I have always been God; there can be no
> others. I alone am the Lord; only I can rescue you. I promised
> to save you, and I kept my promise. You are my witnesses
> that no other god did this. I, the Lord, have spoken. I am God
> now and for ever. No one can snatch you from me or stand
> in my way.

ISAIAH 43:10–13

Later on, God says, 'But I wipe away your sins because of who I am. And so, I will forget the wrongs you have done' (v. 25).

Because of who God is and his great love for each one of us, he forgives us and forgets the wrongs we have done. In light of that, what do you want to say to God about 'Love keeps no record of wrongs'?

If you are in the middle of a difficult situation right now, in which you are being bullied, have been wronged or are recovering after a wrong has been sorted out, God is with you and loves you. Tell him how you are feeling. Remember that it's OK to be angry with God if that's how you feel—Jonah got very cross with God.

It's also important to say that if you are having a problem with a bully but have never told a grown-up, then you should do so. Ask God to give you the courage to tell your story now.

Tell him what you'd like to say. Ask him what you need to ask. Be quiet and listen to what God wants to say to you.

Love tough

Living in God's ways means that we have to 'love tough' and choose to be different. How will you live this out this week? Perhaps there is someone you have argued with or someone who has hurt you and you're finding it hard to let go of the hurt. Talk to God about whether you are 'keeping a record of wrongs' that you don't need to keep, and how you can 'love tough' in this situation.

If you are facing a situation of bullying that needs to be addressed, talk with God about this situation.

What if you realise that you are bullying others and you need help to deal with it? Talk together and pray about what you need to do. The organisation Kidscape has advice for parents who suspect or know that their child is a bully; details can be found on page 108.

＊

Love does not rejoice in evil but rejoices in the truth

It can be shocking when we see people being happy when bad things happen, or not standing up for what's right. We sometimes see pictures on the news of people celebrating when others have been hurt by bombs or fighting. I wonder if you've seen this and how you feel about it. Perhaps you have done something similar yourself: maybe you've laughed or been pleased when you've seen someone make a mistake or get hurt (especially when you think they deserve it). In this chapter we will explore what it means not to rejoice in evil but to delight in the goodness of God's love and truth.

How wide

There was once a man called Zacchaeus who lived in the town of Jericho. Zacchaeus worked as a taxman. He collected money from people to give to the government. He would often charge more than the real rate and keep the extra money for himself, so Zacchaeus was rich—but he had no friends.

One day, Zacchaeus heard that Jesus was in town. Everyone was excited. Crowds gathered. Everyone wanted to catch a glimpse of the famous Jesus. Zacchaeus wanted to see him too.

But there were so many people that Zacchaeus just couldn't see through or past or round all the people. He was getting worried that he would miss out, until he looked up and realised that ahead on the road was a tall, tall tree. The idea blossomed in Zacchaeus's mind. He could climb the tree. Then he would be able to see Jesus.

Being someone who wasn't very tall made climbing the tree very tricky. Reaching up to grab the branches and hauling himself upwards made his arms hurt. He puffed and panted and panted and puffed, and finally he did it. He was up in the tree with a great view of the road. 'YES!' he thought to himself.

There was Jesus, walking down the road. 'It's funny, really,' thought Zacchaeus. 'He's just a man.' Before he knew it, Jesus was underneath the tree, but he didn't just keep walking. He stopped! 'Zacchaeus, come down. I want to come and stay with you tonight,' Jesus said.

Zacchaeus nearly fell out of the tree. 'Did he see me from down the road?' he thought. 'How does he know my name? He wants to come to my house! Why?' Everyone around started frowning and grumbling. 'That's so unfair. Zacchaeus is a thief.'

'Why is Jesus going with that sinner?'

'How dare he?'

Later on, Jesus spoke to his host: 'Zacchaeus, today you and your family have been saved, because you are a true son of Abraham. The Son of Man came to look for and to save people who are lost.'

No one knew what was said or done in Zacchaeus's house, but later that day they heard Zacchaeus promise to give back all the money he had taken, and more.

RETOLD FROM LUKE 19:1–10

How long

Early in the morning, Jesus went into the temple. People came to him, so he sat down and started teaching them.

While he was there, the religious teachers, the Pharisees, dragged a woman in front of Jesus. They said, 'Teacher, this woman has been unfaithful to her husband. She was found in bed with a man she's not married to. The law of Moses says she should be stoned to death because of her sin. What do you say?'

Jesus' reply astonished them. He said nothing! He simply bent over and started writing on the ground with his finger.

'Teacher!' the Pharisees said again. 'What about this woman's sin of unfaithfulness? Should she be stoned to death?'

Jesus continued his writing.

The Pharisees kept on at Jesus, asking and pushing him for a response. Finally, he stood up and said, 'Go ahead and stone her! Just so long as those throwing the stones have never sinned.' With that he bent over again and continued his writing. Quietly, older people in the crowd got up and left. Then, one by one, everyone else silently moved away until finally Jesus and the woman were there alone.

Jesus stood up. 'Where is everyone?' he asked her. 'Isn't anyone left to accuse you?'

'No, sir,' the woman answered.

'Then I won't accuse you either. Go home now, but don't sin any more.'

RETOLD FROM JOHN 8:2–11

How high

Many years ago, when I had just started senior school, there was a boy in my class called Henry. I think you could describe him as a challenging young man. I'd struck up an unlikely friendship with him when we sat on the same bench in Science and melted Bic biros in the Bunsen burner. But there was another side to Henry. He would walk round the class and when he came to someone he didn't like, sadly he would hit them. The first time he did it, I remember feeling shocked. I don't think I'd come across this kind of behaviour before and I didn't like the idea that he hit people for fun.

One day, Henry went beyond his previous bad behaviour when he locked our English teacher in the cupboard and removed the key. How do you think you would have responded if this had happened in your class?

In my class, some people thought it was brilliant, to have the teacher out of the way and not to have a lesson.

Some people were frightened of Henry and just sat still, hoping he wouldn't notice them.

Some people tried to talk Henry into giving the key back so that we could let the teacher out.

Some people went to get help from another teacher.

I can't remember exactly how the incident ended, except that neither Henry nor the English teacher came back to school. The incident has stayed with me, I think, because of the different reactions from people. Some of us worked to get the teacher out and stop Henry hitting people he didn't like, but there were some people who thought the whole thing was a big joke and were happy to have time without a teacher.

Have you ever experienced anything similar?

In our 'How wide' and 'How long' stories, what strikes you about the way Jesus responds in love, not rejoicing in evil but delighting in the truth? What do you think the truth is that the story speaks of? Do you notice that, in these stories, 'evil' is ordinary everyday sin? What do you think about that?

How deep

John 3:21 says, 'Everyone who lives by the truth will come to the light, because they want others to know that God is really the one doing what they do.'

What do you want to say to God about 'Love does not rejoice in evil but delights in the truth'? Tell him what you'd like to say. Ask him what you need to ask. Be quiet and listen to what God wants to say to you.

Love tough

Living in God's ways means that we have to 'love tough' and choose to be different. Talk with God about this and ask him how you can 'love tough', rejecting evil and wrong ways and delighting in the truth of God's love.

Love always protects

'Love always protects' can seem like a big fat lie when we see on the news all the bad things that happen. Today we will explore what it means and how we can rely on God's great protective love.

How wide

A long, long time ago, God said to one of his prophets, 'I called my son out of Egypt.' This is how that promise came true:

After the wise men had visited baby Jesus and had returned to their country without going back to King Herod in Jerusalem, an angel from God appeared to Joseph in a dream. 'Get up, Joseph!' the angel said. 'Hurry—you must get up and leave the area. Take Mary and the baby into Egypt. You'll be safe there. Stay there until I come again and tell you that it's safe to return. Herod is mad, and in his fury he is looking for the child. He wants to kill him. You must leave.'

That very night, while it was still dark, Joseph got up and roused Mary. 'Come, we must go,' he said. He told her about the dream and what the angel had said.

They travelled to Egypt and lived there until they heard that Herod had died. The angel appeared to Joseph again and told him it was safe for the family to return to the land of Israel.

RETOLD FROM MATTHEW 2:13–15

How long

It was night-time. Jesus had just finished praying and was talking with his disciples when they heard people approaching. A large mob armed with swords and clubs, led by Judas the betrayer, came to arrest Jesus on the orders of the religious leaders and chief priest. They all knew the special signal.

Judas walked boldly straight up to Jesus. 'Teacher,' he greeted him, then kissed him.

'Friend,' Jesus replied, 'why are you here?'

The mob of men grabbed Jesus roughly and arrested him. In the confusion, Peter took out his sword. Trying to protect Jesus, he struck out at the men.

'Aaarghh!' came a scream. It was the servant of the high priest. He was kneeling down, blood pouring from a wound, with his ear cut off.

'Stop!' Jesus instructed Peter. 'Put your sword away. Anyone who lives by violence and fighting will themselves die by violence and fighting. Don't you realise that I could ask my Father for more than twelve armies of angels to come and fight for me, and he would send them? But it can't be this way. The scriptures written about me would not come true otherwise.'

Then Jesus spoke to the mob: 'Why do you come with swords and clubs to arrest me like a dangerous criminal? Day after day I sat and taught in the temple, but you didn't come to arrest me there. But this is how it must be, so that what the prophets wrote would come true.'

As the mob took Jesus away, all the disciples left him and ran away.

RETOLD FROM MATTHEW 26:47–56

How high

In what ways do our 'How wide' and 'How long' stories show protective love in action? What do you think God is saying about 'Love always protects' in these stories?

There are often stories on the news about bad things that happen in our world and it can seem as if love does not always protect people from harm, with many crimes happening. This can be hard to understand or can even frighten us. Sometimes, grown-ups feel guilty or sad if something happens to their child and they weren't there to protect them. Everyone has choices about how to behave and what to do, and sometimes people make choices that God wouldn't want them to make (that's really what 'sin' is), so that there are consequences for other people too. But even when very bad things are happening, God is still with his people in the situation. There were many examples of this on 11 September 2001. Terrorist attacks in the USA led to the death of many people, but lots of the survivors said that they had known and experienced God with them on that day.

One thing is certain: 'Love always protects' is *not* about wrongly covering up the sins of another person if a crime is committed. It may be possible to offer protection to a victim by speaking out the truth, rather than protecting a perpetrator or bully by staying silent. This can be hard, because we may be afraid of the consequences, but how might our 'How wide' or 'How long' stories give you peace and courage?

1 Peter 1:5 tells us, 'You have faith in God, whose power will protect you until the last day. Then he will save you, just as he has always planned to do.' It could be that this type of protection is about God's ultimate love and justice in Jesus, who stood before God, for our sins, so that we would be protected from the punishment we really deserve. This is shown in Romans 8:1–2, which says, 'If you belong to Christ Jesus, you won't be punished. The Holy Spirit will give you life that comes from Christ Jesus and will set you free from sin and death.' What do you think about this right now?

How deep

What do you want to say to God about 'Love always protects'? Tell God what you'd like to say. Ask him what you need to ask. Be quiet and listen to what God wants to say to you.

In Paul's letter to the Ephesians, he encourages us to put on God's armour, to protect us spiritually from evil. As you read the verses below, imagine you are putting on the spiritual armour and make this your prayer for today.

> *Be ready! Let the truth be like a belt around your waist, and*
> *let God's justice protect you like armour. Your desire to tell*
> *the good news about peace should be like shoes on your feet.*
> *Let your faith be like a shield, and you will be able to stop all*
> *the flaming arrows of the evil one. Let God's saving power be*
> *like a helmet, and for a sword use God's message that comes*
> *from the Spirit.*

EPHESIANS 6:14–17

Love tough

> *Then you will say to the Lord, 'You are my fortress, my place*
> *of safety; you are my God, and I trust you.'*

PSALM 91:2

Living in God's ways means that we have to 'love tough' and choose to be different. Talk with God about this and ask him how you can 'love tough', trusting in God's protection through Jesus and speaking out to protect others when you know it's right, even if it's hard.

＊

Love always trusts

Trust and trustworthiness are talked about a lot in the Bible as important qualities. In this chapter we will explore what it means to trust and how we can show God's great love to others when we are trustworthy.

How wide

Jesus was entering the town of Capernaum when an army officer came up to him and said, 'Lord, my servant is at home in terrible pain. He can't move because it's so bad.'

'I will go and heal him,' Jesus replied immediately.

But the officer stopped him. 'Lord, I'm not good enough for you to come into my house. Just give the order here and my servant will be well again. In the army I have officers who give me orders, and I have soldiers who take my orders. That's how it is. To one I say "Go!" and he goes; to another I say "Come!" and he comes. I can say to my servant, "Do this!" and he will do it.'

Jesus was astonished at the officer's words. He turned to the crowd and said, 'I tell you that in all my travels in Israel I have never found anyone with this much faith!' Then he turned back to the officer: 'Go home. Your faith has made it happen.'

At that very moment back at the house, the servant got up, fully restored.

RETOLD FROM MATTHEW 8:5–13

How long

The whole town had turned out to see Jesus, it seemed. Everyone was out to welcome him.

'Excuse me… please let me through… excuse me…' Jairus was desperate to get to Jesus. Finally he was there in front of him. 'Please, Lord, my only daughter is very sick. She's dying. Please come, please save her, she's only twelve years old,' he begged.

'Lead me to her,' Jesus answered.

They made their way through the crowd, but there were so many people that it was a slow journey. Fearful for his child's life, Jairus did his best to keep Jesus moving towards his home.

Suddenly Jesus stopped. 'Who touched me?' he asked, looking into the faces of those around him.

'Lord, there are so many people,' Peter said.

'Yes, but I felt power go from me,' Jesus replied.

Trembling, a woman stepped forward and knelt before Jesus. 'My Lord,' she explained, 'I have been bleeding for twelve years. All my money has gone on doctors and not one of them has made me well, but when I heard you were coming, I knew you could heal me. I thought, if I could just touch your cloak, then I would be healed. Please don't be angry with me.'

Jesus smiled compassionately and said, 'Your faith has healed you. Go in God's peace.'

While Jesus was still speaking, someone arrived and said to Jairus, 'Your daughter has died. Do not trouble the Master any further.' Jesus heard this and said, 'Do not be afraid. Only have faith and she will be saved.' When they reached Jairus's house, Jesus took the girl by the hand and said, 'Child, get up.' Her spirit returned and she got up at that very moment.

RETOLD FROM LUKE 8:40–55

How high

Have you ever had to trust someone totally?

I remember the very first time I went abseiling at Guide camp. I had never had to wear a harness before. I had never climbed up so high before. I remember watching the man clip the girls in front of me on to the rope and talk them through going over the edge, and how to feed the rope through so that they got to the bottom. Then it was my turn. I remember watching him clip on the rope as he had done at least ten times before. Then he told me to go to the edge and lean back.

I had no choice but to trust him. I had seen my friends go before. Some of them had clearly been scared but some of them had happily jumped and bounced their way to the ground. I think I went for something in the middle—starting off slowly and carefully and doing a few bounces on my way down.

I wonder if trusting God is a bit like this. Often we start off carefully but then learn that God is trustworthy and keeps his promises, so we can afford a jump and a bounce! Talk together about a time when you have trusted God. What was it like?

I wonder what the examples of the army officer, Jairus and the woman from our 'How wide' and 'How long' stories show you about trust. Talk together about this.

Were you ever in a situation where you did something that broke someone's trust in you? Perhaps you said you would be somewhere, then didn't go, or stayed out longer than you should, or lied about who you were seeing. How did it feel when that happened? How did you go about rebuilding trust?

Being trustworthy is part of showing God's great love to others. What do you think this means for the way you behave as a friend?

Sometimes it can be hard for us to trust God when others around us don't know or trust him. How do you feel when this happens to you? What do you think God wants to say to you about it?

How deep

Psalm 89:2 says, 'God's love can always be trusted, and his faithfulness lasts as long as the heavens,' but maybe you find it difficult to trust God. What do you want to say to God about 'Love always trusts'? Tell him what you'd like to say. Ask him what you need to ask. Be quiet and listen to what God wants to say to you.

Love tough

When Jesus sent the disciples out to spread his message, he told them to take nothing with them (not even so much as a set of spare shoes). Therefore they had to trust God for everything and rely on the generosity and hospitality of people who were willing to share. (You can read about it in Matthew 10:5–15.)

Living in God's ways means that we have to 'love tough' and choose to be different. Talk with God about this and ask him how you can 'love tough', trusting him even when the people around you don't.

Love always hopes

Love always hopes and never gives in to despair even when, to human eyes, there is no hope. God's great love is far bigger and greater than we can see. In this chapter we'll explore how love can keep hoping and not give up.

How wide

Anna talked with God a lot. God talked with Anna a lot, too. Anna was now 84 years old but when she was a younger woman she had been married. She remembered her husband with great fondness and a tinge of sadness. They had only been married for seven years before her husband had died. But now, night and day, she served God in the temple by praying. She often worshipped God by going without food for a short time.

Anna was there on the day that Mary and Joseph brought their baby to the temple to say 'thank you' to God for his birth. She praised God for Jesus and spoke about him to everyone who was hoping for Jerusalem to be set free.

RETOLD FROM LUKE 2:36–38

How long

It was the sabbath, the holy day when Jews were to do no work. Jesus and his disciples had already had a confrontation with some of the religious leaders and Pharisees about what it means to work on the sabbath. The Pharisees were looking for an excuse to get rid of

Jesus, so they followed him and watched him, hoping he would do something wrong.

They followed as Jesus went into one of the Jewish meeting places, where among the people was a man born with a damaged hand. The Pharisees saw an opportunity! 'Is it right to heal someone on the sabbath?' they asked.

Jesus answered, 'If you owned a sheep that fell into a ditch on the sabbath, wouldn't you lift it out? People are worth so much more than sheep, so yes, it is right to do good on the sabbath.' Then he turned to the man. 'Hold out your hand,' he instructed. As the man raised his hand, it became healthy—completely better!

The Pharisees were fuming. Hurriedly they left, beginning to make plans to kill Jesus. Word about their plans got back to Jesus, so he left the area, with large crowds following him. He healed everyone who was ill, but warned them not to tell anyone about him. So it was that God's promise came true, just as God's messenger Isaiah had said:

'Here is my chosen servant! I love him, and he pleases me. I will give him my Spirit. He will bring justice to the nations. He won't shout or yell or call out in the streets. He won't break a damaged or bent reed, nor will he snuff out a dying flame, but he will make sure that justice is done. All nations will place their hope in him.'

RETOLD FROM MATTHEW 12:9–21

How high

What's the thing that you have hoped for most? Talk together about hopes that you have had. Perhaps it was for a particular present for Christmas or your birthday. Perhaps you have hoped for a baby brother or sister. Perhaps you've hoped for someone to get better when they've been ill. Perhaps you hope to see a loved one who has died in heaven one day.

'Love always hopes' asks us to think about the hope that we have to be with God for eternity because of Jesus. In our 'How wide' story, Anna had been waiting in the temple for years, praying for the Messiah whose coming had been foretold hundreds of years before. When you think about your hopes for the future, do they include the hope that Jesus will return to earth or that you will be with God for ever in heaven?

Does the 'How long' story help or hinder you in thinking about 'Love always hopes'? What do you think Isaiah might mean when he says, 'All nations will place their hope in him'?

It is easy for us to look with human eyes at situations and be overwhelmed with hopelessness when we can't easily see a way through. But God's great love goes beyond our need for answers here and now and can enable us to keep our hope in God's everlasting presence and love. Talk together about how God's great love gives you a hope for the future. God talked about this with the prophet Jeremiah in the Old Testament: 'I will bless you with a future filled with hope—a future of success, not of suffering' (Jeremiah 29:11).

How deep

One of the big questions that people often ask about life is 'What happens after we die?' What we think and hope about this question can affect the way we live our lives.

There is an amazing story in the Gospels about the time when Jesus' friend Lazarus became ill and died. Lazarus had two sisters, Mary and Martha, who were also friends of Jesus. When the story starts, Jesus is in another town. He knows that Lazarus is ill and will die but he isn't worried because through this event he can demonstrate God's greatness. Sure enough, by the time he gets to Lazarus' home town, his friend is dead and the two sisters are devastated. Martha comes out of the village to meet with Jesus and they talk together about who Jesus is and the hope for life after death. When he asks if she believes him, she replies, 'Yes, Lord! I believe that you are Christ, the Son of God. You are the one we hoped would come into the world' (John 11:27).

To discover what happened to Lazarus, you can explore the whole story in John chapter 11.

What do you want to say to God about 'Love always hopes'? Tell God what you'd like to say. Ask him what you need to ask. Be quiet and listen to what God wants to say to you.

Write a prayer or poem about your hope in God.

Love tough

> *At that time, people will say, 'The Lord has saved us! Let's celebrate. We waited and hoped—now our God is here.'*

ISAIAH 25:9

Living in God's ways means that we have to 'love tough' and choose to be different. Talk with God about this and ask him how you can 'love tough', hoping in an eternal future with him, even though it's hard to imagine with all the difficult things we see in the world now.

Love always perseveres

When have you done something that needed you to persevere—to keep on going without giving up, even when you felt too tired or just unable to continue? Our stories today show us times when people didn't give up, even in the face of difficulties, and we will explore what this shows us about God's great love.

How wide

When Jesus was born in Bethlehem, Herod was king of that land. During that time, some travellers, known as wise men, came to Jerusalem after a long journey. They came to Herod and asked, 'Where is the child born to be the king of the Jews? We saw his star in the east and have come to worship him. We thought he would be in your palace.'

Herod was taken aback. Who was this baby they spoke of? A new king? But *he* was the king of the Jews!

Herod could find no one else in Jerusalem who could shed any light on the matter, even though he consulted many wise and religious people in the city. This worried him. Finally he talked with the chief priests and the Jewish teachers.

'Where will the Messiah be born?' he asked.

'In Bethlehem,' they told him. 'The prophets of old foretold it.'

Herod was concerned. Herod was cunning. He secretly called the visitors to him. 'Go to Bethlehem and find the child. When you find him, send word to me so that I might go and worship him too.'

Leaving Jerusalem, the wise men were excited about following the star. It led them to the place where the child was, and stopped.

They went into the house and saw the child with his mother. They knelt down and worshipped him and presented their gifts of gold, frankincense and myrrh. All too soon it was time to go home, but the wise men had been warned in a dream not to return to Herod, so they began their long journey back on a different road, avoiding Jerusalem.

RETOLD FROM MATTHEW 2:1–12

How long

One day the tax collectors and sinners were all crowding round, listening to Jesus. But the religious teachers started grumbling. 'Why is Jesus friendly with these sinners?' one said. 'Yes, he even shares food with them!' said another. Then Jesus told them some stories.

'If you have a flock of 100 sheep, and one of them gets lost, what will you do? Surely you will leave the 99 safely in the field and go searching for that sheep. You'll keep looking until you find it. Right? And when you find it, you will put it on your shoulders and carry it home. Then, in your deep joy at finding it, you will call your friends and neighbours and invite them over for a celebration.

'You know, it's the same in heaven. There is more joy when one sinner turns to God than over 99 good people.'

Jesus told them another story.

'If a woman has ten silver coins and she loses one, what will she do? Won't she light a lamp and look for the coin? She'll even sweep the floor and keep searching carefully until she finds it. Then, when it's found, she will call her friends and neighbours and say, "Let's celebrate! I've found the coin I lost."'

Jesus finished, 'In the same way, God's angels are so happy when even one person turns to him.'

RETOLD FROM LUKE 15:1–10

How high

Talk together about times when you've had to persevere—to keep going and not give up.

I remember the time in the autumn of 2011 when I found out I'd got a place in the 2012 London Marathon. I was really excited on one hand and very scared on the other. I had never run a full marathon before. Although I knew I could run for about 15 miles and I hoped I could keep going for the full 26.2, I wasn't 100 per cent sure I could.

Through the winter and early spring, I trained hard, running miles and miles and miles, building up the strength and endurance to be able to complete the marathon. On the day, I knew that (barring serious injury) I would finish. I hoped to finish in around four hours, but my goal was really just to get to the end and enjoy the race as much as I could. There are things I remember about the day, like passing the Cutty Sark, turning on to Tower Bridge, seeing my family in the crowd, and hearing the woman on the Embankment who shouted, 'Go on, Yvonne, you're doing great! Nearly there, love, nearly there.' (I didn't know her, but I had my name on my vest.) I also remember Big Ben striking as I came past, but after that I have no memory of getting to the finish line. In fact, when I was in Westminster later in the year, I looked around and didn't even know what direction I had run in after Big Ben.

Running the marathon did hurt. My whole body hurt in a way I hadn't experienced before. But I knew I could and would get to the end, and the fact that I did fills me with pride.

I love it that God's love has the perseverance, patience and endurance never to give up, not to get tired, not to wonder if it's strong enough to finish, and not to forget how it got to where it was going! Look again at the 'How wide' and 'How long' stories and think about how they demonstrate perseverance and endurance.

How deep

What do you want to say to God about 'Love always perseveres'? Tell God what you'd like to say. Ask him what you need to ask. Be quiet and listen to what God wants to say to you.

Psalm 27:14 says, 'Wait for the Lord; be strong, and let your heart take courage; wait for the Lord!' (NRSV).

Love tough

Living in God's ways means that we have to 'love tough' and choose to be different. Talk with God about this and ask him how you can 'love tough', persevering and remembering Romans 8:37–39:

> *In everything we have won more than a victory because of Christ who loves us. I am sure that nothing can separate us from God's love—not life or death, not angels or spirits, not the present or the future, and not powers above or powers below. Nothing in all creation can separate us from God's love for us in Christ Jesus our Lord!*

Love never fails

People often let us down, which can make it hard for us to accept that God never lets us down. Good Friday, as it is now known, is where we start in this chapter. Children often ask, 'Why is Good Friday called Good Friday, when it's bad that Jesus died?' In this chapter we will explore how Jesus shows us that God's love is so big that it never fails, even when everything looks dark and far from good.

How wide

Midday came and the sky turned black. Through the dark afternoon Jesus was there on the cross. Nearby, some women, shocked and numb with sadness, were watching. They had followed Jesus on his travels and had helped to look after him and his disciples. They were heartbroken but they stayed close by.

Mary, his mother, was there, supported in her grief by her sister and other men and women who followed Jesus. 'This man is now your son,' Jesus called to her, and to the disciple John he said, 'She is now your mother.' Mary went home with John and lived in his care from then on.

When three o'clock came, Jesus shouted out, '*Eloi, Eloi, lema sabach-thani*,' which means 'My God, my God, why have you abandoned me?' Then he died. At that exact moment the huge curtain in the temple tore in two from top to bottom.

One of the Roman officers standing in front of Jesus bowed his head. 'He really was the Son of God,' he whispered.

By now it was late afternoon. The Jewish people were getting ready for their sabbath, their holy day, which started when the sun went down. Once the sabbath started, the Jews were at rest and jobs like burying a dead body could not be done.

A man named Joseph, from the town of Arimathea, was a highly respected member of the Jewish council but he also believed in Jesus. Joseph went to Pilate and asked, 'Give me the body of Jesus so that I can lay him in a tomb before the sabbath comes.'

'Already? Is he really dead?' Pilate was surprised. An officer came from Skull Hill and confirmed the report. Jesus was really dead and ready to be buried. 'You may lay him in your tomb,' Pilate told Joseph.

Returning to Skull Hill with a linen cloth, Joseph took down Jesus' body from the cross. Carefully he wrapped the body and took it to the tomb that had been cut into a solid rock. Then he rolled a big stone against the entrance of the tomb.

Mary Magdalene and some of the other women followed and saw where the body was laid, so they knew where to return after the sabbath with the burial spices. On the sabbath they rested, just as God had commanded in the old law.

RETOLD FROM MARK 15:33–47; JOHN 19:25–27

How long

Very early on Sunday morning, before dawn, Mary Magdalene went back to the tomb. She was planning to prepare Jesus' body for burial, but as she came near she could see that the stone had been rolled away from the entrance.

'Oh no!' She turned and ran to the place where Simon Peter and John were. 'Peter, John, come! They have taken the Lord from the tomb. I don't know where they have put him.'

The men headed straight for the tomb, sprinting as fast as they could. John arrived first and saw that Mary was right—the stone had been rolled away—but John could not go in. Running up, panting hard, Peter didn't hesitate. Looking at John, he went in and saw the strips of linen cloth, lying neatly. He stood amazed, trying desperately to make sense of what he saw and what he felt in his heart.

Following Peter's lead, John entered the tomb and, when he saw the linen cloths, he believed. The two men ran back to tell the other disciples what they had seen.

Again, Mary stayed. Confused, upset, unknowing, she could do nothing but cry. She moved towards the place where the body had been. As she peeped inside, through her tears she saw two angels sitting there.

'Why are you crying?' they asked.

'The body of my Lord has been taken away! I don't know where he is. If you know, please tell me,' she replied. As she spoke the words, her grief flooded out and she moved back away from the empty tomb.

Turning, she bumped into a man. 'Why are you crying? Who are you looking for?' he said gently.

'Sir, his body is gone, taken away. If you know where he is, please tell me. Tell me so that I can go to him.'

The man spoke again: 'Mary!'

'Oh! Teacher!' she replied.

'Don't hold on to me!' Jesus told her. 'I have not yet gone to my Father. Tell my disciples that I am going to the God who is my Father and yours.' Mary went and told her story to the disciples.

Unsure what to make of the day's events and still afraid of the Jewish leaders, the disciples locked themselves in a room when the evening came. Suddenly, Jesus stood among them. He greeted them. 'Peace be with you,' he said. He showed them his hands and side with the scars from the cross. They realised it was him and their happiness and courage were restored.

'I am sending you, just as my Father sent me,' Jesus said. Then he breathed on them and said, 'Receive the Holy Spirit. If you forgive anyone's sins, they will be forgiven, but if you don't forgive their sins, they will not be forgiven.'

RETOLD FROM JOHN 20:1–21

How high

I wonder if you've ever seen or felt something was just 'too big'?

When I was a child, on one occasion we went on a family outing to Whipsnade Zoo. We had linked up with my aunt, uncle and two baby cousins, one of whom was a toddler, just learning to walk and talk. In those days, the first thing you saw when you entered Whipsnade was the elephant enclosure, and we headed straight for it, excited to see the elephants out and about. But as we drew near, my young cousin got agitated and was saying, 'Too big!' She kept repeating, 'Too big, no el'phant, too big!'

My aunt explained that she had a small cuddly elephant at home, so the sight of a real elephant up close was too much for her. It was just 'too big'!

I wonder if sometimes God's love feels just 'too big' for us humans. When Paul said, 'Love never fails,' he meant it. On the cross, when God the Son cried out to God the Father, 'Why have you abandoned me?' it looked as if Jesus' enemies had won. But even when he was feeling abandoned, Jesus was concerned for his mother. He wanted her to know that she wasn't abandoned and that she had someone who would take care of her. How do you think Mary felt when she heard him looking after her in this way?

God's enemies, even death, had not won. God was not beaten. In our 'How long' story, we see the next part of that never-failing love.

Love never fails. Never means 'at no time, past or present'. At no time has God's love failed. God loves you and me so, so much that he was prepared to sacrifice his only son so that our sins would be forgiven and we could be reunited with God for ever.

Human love can fail. We can feel let down, disappointed or unfulfilled by human love, and this can cloud our thinking and our understanding of God's love. But I encourage you to think about that phrase for a little while: 'At no time has God's love failed.' Even if you feel that human love has failed or does fail, God's love has never and does not. This is a very big idea to wonder about.

How deep

Jesus is the living, breathing example that God's tough love never fails. In John 11:25–26, Jesus asks his friend, Martha, if she believes him when he says, 'I am the resurrection and the life. The one who believes in me will live, even though they die; and whoever lives by believing in me will never die' (NIV). How do you feel about this right now?

What do you want to say to God about 'Love never fails'? Tell God what you'd like to say. Ask him what you need to ask. Be quiet and listen to what God wants to say to you.

Love tough

Living in God's ways means that we have to 'love tough' and choose to be different. Talk with God about this and ask him how you can 'love tough' by living in his unfailing love.

Love your neighbour as you love yourself

What does loving yourself look like? If you cared for others just as well as you look after and care for yourself, what would the world be like? In this chapter we'll explore these questions a bit further.

How wide

One day Jesus was asked a question: 'Teacher, what must I do to have eternal life?'

'What is written in the scriptures?' Jesus answered. 'How do you understand what they say?'

'Well, the scriptures say that you must "Love the Lord you God with all your heart, soul, strength and mind". And they also say, "Love your neighbour as much as you love yourself."'

'Yes, you are right. If you do this you will have eternal life,' Jesus answered.

But the man hadn't finished his questioning. 'Who is my neighbour?' he asked. Jesus answered with a story.

'One day a man was travelling from Jerusalem to Jericho. On the way, robbers attacked him, beat him up, stole his things and ran off, leaving him on the road half dead.

'A priest happened to be travelling the same road, but when he saw the man, he walked by on the other side of the road.

'Later, another person was on the road. He helped at the temple. When he came to the place where the man was, he also crossed the road and walked by.

'Later still, a man from Samaria, a foreign country, came along. He saw the man lying on the road. He felt very sorry for him and went over to him. He washed his wounds and bandaged them before lifting the man up on to his own donkey. The Samaritan led the donkey to an inn, where he hired a room and took the man in. The next morning, he gave the innkeeper more money and asked him to take care of the man, saying, "If you spend more on him than this, I will pay you when I return."'

Then Jesus asked, 'Which of the three was a real neighbour to the man beaten up by the robbers?'

'The one who showed care and helped,' came the reply.

'Then go and do the same!' Jesus said.

RETOLD FROM LUKE 10:25–37

How long

Jesus told another story.

'When the Son of Man comes in his glory with all his angels, he will be king and sit on his royal throne. All the peoples of the world will be brought before him and he will separate them, like the shepherd who separates the sheep and the goats.

'He will place the sheep on his right and the goats on his left. Then the king will say to those on his right, "My father has blessed you! Come and receive the kingdom that was prepared for you before the world was created. When I was hungry, you gave me food. When I was thirsty, you gave me drink. When I was a stranger, you welcomed me. When I was naked, you gave me clothes to wear. When I was sick, you looked after me. When I was in prison, you visited me."

'Those on the right who pleased the Lord will ask, "When did we do that? When did we give you food or drink? When did we welcome you and clothe you or visit you while you were in prison?"

'The king will answer, "Whenever you did this for any of my people, you did it for me."

'Then the king will say to the people on the left, "Get away from me! Leave me now. You are not blessed but are banished by God. Go into the everlasting fire prepared for the devil and his angels. I was hungry but you gave me nothing. I was thirsty but you gave me no drink. I was a stranger and you ignored me. I was naked but you left me unclothed. I was sick but you didn't care. I was in prison and you refused to visit me."

'Then these people will cry out, "When? When did we fail to help you?"

'The king will say to them, "Whenever you failed to help any of my people, no matter how unimportant they seemed to be, then you failed to do it for me."'

Jesus finished by saying, 'They will be punished for ever, but people who lived rightly, with and for God, will have eternal life.'

RETOLD FROM MATTHEW 25:34–46

How high

Talk together and make a list of all the things you do each day to look after yourself and keep your body, mind and spirit healthy and happy. What would happen if you didn't do any one of the things on your list?

Talk together about who is your neighbour. When I was at school, there was a boy in my class called John. John came from a very poor family and was often untidy and dirty. He struggled with lessons and he didn't have any friends, which made him an easy target for bullying. People were often unkind to John, and it was hard to stand out and offer him support, help and a kind word, but some of us tried. Back then, I wouldn't have considered John a 'neighbour' exactly, but he didn't deserve what some people said about and to him. I wonder how I would have felt if our places had been switched.

Is there someone in your school like John? How does God want you to show them his love?

All the way back in the Old Testament, when God first set out how people should behave towards each other, it says, 'Stop being angry and don't try to take revenge. I am the Lord, and I command you to love others as much as you love yourself' (Leviticus 19:18). What do you think about this as a rule for life?

How deep

What do you want to say to God about 'Love your neighbour as you love yourself'? Tell him what you'd like to say. Ask him what you need to ask. Be quiet and listen to what God wants to say to you.

Romans 13:8–10 says:

> *Let love be your only debt! If you love others, you have done all that the Law demands. In the Law there are many commands, such as, 'Be faithful in marriage. Do not murder. Do not steal. Do not want what belongs to others.' But all these are summed up in the command that says, 'Love others as much as you love yourself.' No one who loves others will harm them. So love is all that the Law demands.*

Write or draw a prayer or poem about 'Love your neighbour' today.

Love tough

Think what a beautiful place the world would be if everyone loved their neighbour as they love themselves.

Living in God's ways means that we have to 'love tough' and choose to be different. Talk with God about this and ask him how you can 'love tough' by loving neighbours as much as you love yourself.

☀

Love the Lord your God with all your heart, soul, mind and strength

Your 'heart, soul, mind and strength' represent all that you are—spiritually, emotionally, physically and mentally. In this chapter we explore what it will look like if God is asking us to use every part of ourselves to love him.

How wide

A man came to Jesus and asked him, 'Teacher, what good thing must I do to have eternal life?'

Jesus looked at him. 'Why are you asking me what is good? Only God is good. If you want eternal life, you must obey his commandments.'

'But which ones?' the man pushed.

'Well, do not murder. Be faithful in marriage. Do not steal. Don't tell lies about others. Respect your father and mother, and love others as much as you love yourself.'

'But I do all those. What else?' the man replied.

The man couldn't help thinking that this 'God stuff' was easy-peasy. That is, until Jesus spoke again: 'If you want to be perfect, go and sell everything you own. Give the money to the poor, and you will have riches in heaven. Then, come and be my follower.'

This made the man very sad, because he was very rich. He went away from Jesus.

Some of the disciples asked Jesus about what he had said. Jesus replied, 'You must realise that it is terribly hard for rich people to get into heaven. In fact, it is easier for a camel to go through the eye of a needle than it is for a rich person to get into God's kingdom.'

The disciples were taken aback at this answer, so they asked Jesus, 'How can anyone be saved, then?'

'There are some things that people cannot do, but God can do anything,' he answered.

'But don't forget that we have left everything to be your followers! What will we get, then?' Peter blurted out.

'Yes, all of you have become my followers,' said Jesus. 'So in the eternal world, when the Son of Man sits on his glorious throne, I promise that you will sit on twelve thrones to be judges of the twelve tribes of Israel. All who have given up their home or land, brothers, sisters, father, mother or children, for me, will be given a hundred times as much. They will also have eternal life. But many who are now first will be last and many who are last will be first.

'The kingdom of heaven is like what happens when someone finds treasure hidden in a field. He buries it again and then goes to sell everything he has to buy the field. The kingdom of heaven is also like what happens when a shop owner is looking for fine pearls. After finding a really valuable one, the owner goes and sells everything he has so that he can buy that one precious pearl.'

RETOLD FROM MATTHEW 19:16–30

How long

One time, a religious Pharisee came to test Jesus. 'Teacher, what is the most important commandment in the law?' he asked.

Jesus, knowing it was a tricky question, answered, 'Love the Lord your God with all your heart, soul and mind. The second most important commandment is to love others as much as you love yourself. All the law of Moses and the books of the prophets are based on these commandments.'

RETOLD FROM MATTHEW 22:35–40

How high

I love to run, and I have run marathons. I buy good trainers and kit, so that I will feel comfortable. I read books and magazines that help me plan my training, tell me which are the right foods to eat, and give me something to look at while I'm resting (which is an important part of marathon training). And, of course, I spend time actually running. When I'm in the middle of marathon training, I can cover around 100 miles a month, which takes about 16 hours of running time. To me, it's worth the time because, when I run a race, I'm confident that I have put in the training that will enable me to complete the distance. It's often hard, but the sense of achievement, especially when I beat a previous time, makes it worthwhile.

Do you play a musical instrument or a sport? Do you love dancing or art? How much time do you spend doing your hobby?

It is widely quoted that to become an expert, master or champion, you need to spend 10,000 hours doing that thing, whether it's sport, dancing, music or another skill that you want to become an expert in. Ten thousand hours is a long time! If you put in only one hour a day, it would take over 27 years to become expert.

I wonder if this type of investment in time and effort is what God is talking about when he asks us to love him with all our heart, soul, mind and strength. Talk together about what you think it would look like to love God in this way.

How deep

2 John:5–6 says, 'I am writing to tell you to love each other, which is the first thing you were told to do. Love means that we do what God tells us. And from the beginning, he told you to love him.'

What do you want to say to God about loving him 'with all your heart, soul, mind and strength'? Tell God what you'd like to say. Ask him what you need to ask. Be quiet and listen to what God wants to say to you.

What is your prayer today? Write or draw it.

Love tough

What sort of world do you think it would be if everyone put God and his ways first? Living in God's ways means that we have to 'love tough' and choose to be different. Talk with God about this and ask him how you can 'love tough' with all that you are.

Love your enemies

I think that 'Love your enemies' is probably the hardest of the love commands. It goes against our every instinct, to love and be kind to those who are unkind and cruel to us. But this is God's big tough love we're talking about, which demands God's outrageous grace to be lived out through us.

How wide

Jesus was speaking to a large crowd.

He said, 'Listen to me. This is what I say to those who will listen. Love your enemies and be kind to everyone who hates you. Ask God to bless anyone who torments you, and pray for everyone who is cruel to you. If someone slaps you on one cheek, don't stop that person from slapping you on the other cheek. If someone wants to take your coat, give them your shirt as well. Give to everyone who asks and don't ask people to give back what they have taken from you. Treat others just as you want to be treated.

'If you only love someone who loves you back, will God praise you? Everyone loves people who love them. If you are only kind to people who are kind to you, will God be pleased with you for that? Even sinners are kind to people who are kind to them. If you lend money only to someone you think will pay you back, will God be pleased with you for that? Even sinners lend to sinners because they think they will get it back.

'But love your enemies and be good to them. Lend without expecting to be paid back. Then you will get a great reward, and you will be the true children of God in heaven. He is good even to people who are unthankful and cruel. Have pity on others, just as your Father has pity on you.'

RETOLD FROM LUKE 6:27–36

How long

Dear friends... Be sincere in your love for others. Hate everything that is evil and hold tight to everything that is good. Love each other as brothers and sisters and honour others more than you do yourself. Never give up. Eagerly follow the Holy Spirit and serve God. Let your hope make you glad. Be patient in time of trouble and never stop praying. Take care of God's needy people and welcome strangers into your home.

Ask God to bless everyone who ill-treats you. Ask him to bless them and not to curse them. When others are happy, be happy with them, and when they are sad, be sad. Be friendly with everyone. Don't be proud and feel that you are cleverer than others. Make friends with ordinary people. Don't ill-treat someone who has ill-treated you. But try to earn the respect of others, and do your best to live in peace with everyone.

Dear friends, don't try to get even. Let God take revenge. In the Scriptures the Lord says, 'I am the one to take revenge and pay them back.' The Scriptures also say, 'If your enemies are hungry, give them something to eat. And if they are thirsty, give them something to drink. This will be the same as piling burning coals on their heads.'

Don't let evil defeat you, but defeat evil with good.

ROMANS 12:9–21

How high

My daughter has some wonderful friends at school, but occasionally they have rows or fall out. One day, she said to me that it's hard to imagine that God loves people who are mean to you or who you struggle with. She feels, in the times of trouble, that God helps her to remember that they still have a good side, even though they may be behaving wrongly towards her at that moment.

As we have seen, loving our enemies is probably the hardest of God's tough love commands to put into practice. There will always be people you don't get on with so well (remember Jesus and the Pharisees and the religious leaders) but to 'love' our enemies actively, especially those who are particularly unkind towards us or who bully us, is really difficult.

Sometimes grown-ups say things like, 'You should forgive and forget.' I think this is too easy to say. When we are feeling pain, uncertainty or fear because of the things others do or say (or don't do), and especially when they don't change their behaviour towards us, the concept of forgiving and forgetting may seem a step too far. This is a normal human reaction, but Jesus does challenge us on our attitude to forgiving.

Peter and Jesus were once talking when Peter asked, 'How many times should I forgive someone who does something wrong to me? Is seven times enough?' Jesus answered, 'Not just seven times, but seventy-seven times!' You can read the full story in Matthew 18:21–35. I wonder if you've noticed that the Lord's Prayer includes the line, 'Forgive us for doing wrong, as we forgive others'.

No one ever said that following Jesus and living God's way was going to be easy, but what might help when you are in a tricky situation? I once worked with someone who was very difficult to get on with and seemed never to be willing to see things from any perspective other than his own. This made office life quite unhappy and difficult for myself and others. It was a struggle to know how to behave towards him when, every day, we didn't know how he was going to behave towards us. Some days it was fine, but other days he was selfish and rude and unreasonable.

One day, I was talking about this situation with a wise Christian friend of mine. She said that when we are struggling to love people in certain situations, we should ask God to help us to see them with his eyes. This really helped me, because when I prayed to see him as God sees him, I saw a man in pain, struggling with his private life, feeling frightened and not knowing how to show others that he cared. Understanding these things helped me to know how to talk to him and behave towards him with greater sympathy.

I wonder what will happen if you ask God to help you to see a difficult person through his eyes, and to love that person with his heart.

How deep

Remember that Jesus said, 'But I tell you to love your enemies and pray for anyone who ill-treats you' (Matthew 5:44). With that in mind, what do you want to say to God about 'Love your enemies'? Tell God what you'd like to say. Ask him what you need to ask. Be quiet and listen to what God wants to say to you.

The words of the Psalms can often comfort and help us because people wrote them to reflect how they were feeling. I wonder if Psalm 40:1–3 might help you if you are in a difficult situation right now:

> *I patiently waited, Lord, for you to hear my prayer. You*
> *listened and pulled me from a lonely pit full of mud and mire.*
> *You let me stand on a rock with my feet firm, and you gave*
> *me a new song, a song of praise to you.*

You could write your own psalm or prayer about how you are feeling today.

Does it help you to remember that none of us deserve God's love and kindness? We are all sinners, but through Jesus we can be in God's presence. 1 Peter 5:10 says, 'But God shows undeserved kindness to everyone. That's why he appointed Christ Jesus to choose you to share in his eternal glory. You will suffer for a while, but God will make you complete, steady, strong, and firm.'

Can you make this your prayer today?

Love tough

'Love your enemies' is a big ask! But living in God's ways means that we have to 'love tough' and choose to be different. Talk with God about this and ask him how you can 'love tough' by loving your enemies.

Love one another as I have loved you

Giving love just as we have received it from God sounds as if it should be easy (if we know what it means to get love, we should be able to give it too), but it never seems to work out quite like that. In this chapter we will explore what loving others as God loves us might look like in practice.

How wide

As the meal ended, Jesus looked around at his friends. His eyes rested on Judas. 'Go, Judas and do what you must do.' Judas got up, took a piece of bread and went out into the night.

After Judas had gone, Jesus spoke to the others. 'Now the Son of Man will be given glory, and he will bring glory to God. Then, after God is given glory because of him, God will bring glory to him, and God will do it very soon.

'My children, I will be with you for a little while longer. Then you will look for me but won't find me. I tell you just as I told the people, "You cannot go where I am going." But I give you a new command. You must love each other, just as I have loved you. If you love each other, everyone will know that you are my disciples.'

'Lord, where are you going?' Simon Peter asked. Jesus replied, 'You can't go where I am going with me now, but later you can.'

'Why, Lord? Why can't I go with you now? I would die for you!'

'Would you, Peter? Would you really die for me?' Jesus asked. 'I tell you for certain that before the cock crows, you will say three times that you don't even know me.'

RETOLD FROM JOHN 13:27–38

How long

My dear friends, we must love each other. Love comes from God, and when we love each other, it shows that we have God's Spirit living in us. Now that we know and believe in Jesus, we are God's children and we know our heavenly Father. We know that God is love. Anyone who doesn't love others doesn't know and has never known God. God showed how much he loves us firstly by bringing Jesus into the world to give us life and secondly by sacrificing his only Son so that our sins are forgiven. Real love isn't our love for God but his love for us (and this is a very big love). Dear friends, since God loves us this much, we *must* love each other.

No one has ever seen the Father God but, if we love each other, God lives in us and his love is truly in our hearts.

God has given us his Spirit. This is how we know that we are one with him, just as he is one with us. God sent his Son to be the Saviour of the world. We saw Jesus and are now telling others about him. God stays one with everyone who openly says that Jesus is the Son of God. That's how we stay one with God and are sure that God loves us.

God is love. If we keep on loving others, we will stay true to God in our hearts and he will stay one with us. If we truly love others and live as Jesus did, bringing God's love, justice, mercy and peace to the world, we won't be worried about dying and being judged. A real love for others will chase all those worries away, because God will know that we have loved as he loves. Thinking about judgement as punishment makes us afraid, but when we really learn to love, we don't need to be afraid of judgement.

We love because God loved us first. If we say we love God but don't love each other, we are liars. We cannot see God, but we can see people. We show our love for God by loving people. After all, God has commanded us, 'Love God and love each other!'

RETOLD FROM 1 JOHN 4:7–21

How high

I can still remember sitting in the school hall at Wenlock Junior School, singing, 'A new commandment I give unto you, that you love one another as I have loved you.' Apart from really liking the tune, I remember that, even though I went to church and knew lots of Bible stories, when I sang this song in the school hall it was like God talking to me as never before. I remember the moment when I realised that if I was going to call myself a Christian, a disciple, a follower of Jesus, then others should be able to tell something about Jesus by the way I behaved. It was like God and me having a conversation, there and then, about what it meant to say that I loved him.

Of course, I don't claim to be anything near perfect at this kind of love. Even though God and I had that conversation, I know there are many times when I ignore it, forget it or just get it wrong, but there are also times when, together, we get it right.

Throughout the chapters in this book, we have explored many of the ways in which God shows us his great big tough love, especially in what Jesus said and did, and how he asks us to share that love with others. We have explored the times when this is easy and when it's hard, and it's often a bit confusing, too. Take a moment to think and talk together about how, in everyday life, you see and feel God's love around you.

How did our 'How wide' and 'How long' stories help or hinder you today?

Sometimes you can know in your head that God is close by and loves you very much, but it can sometimes feel as if he is very far away. It might be helpful to think of the ways in which you show others that you love them, and ask God to do the same for you. For example, you might feel him hugging you or giving you a smile, walking and talking with you or just sitting companionably next to you.

How deep

What do you want to say to God about 'Love one another as I have loved you'? Tell God what you'd like to say. Ask him what you need to ask. Be quiet and listen to what God wants to say to you.

> *Your love is faithful, Lord, and even the clouds in the sky can depend on you. Your decisions are always fair. They are firm like mountains, deep like the sea, and all people and animals are under your care. Your love is a treasure, and everyone finds shelter in the shadow of your wings.*

PSALM 36:5–7

Spend some time thinking about these words and how God's love is pictured there. Write a prayer or poem or draw a picture of how you imagine God's love.

Love tough

Living in God's ways means that we have to 'love tough' and choose to be different. Talk with God about this and ask him how you can 'love tough', loving others as he loves you.

Do you love me?

Having explored so many ways that we can give and receive God's love, in this final chapter we consider our response to Jesus when he asks, 'Do you love me?'

How wide

After they had finished breakfast, Jesus and Simon Peter walked together along the beach. 'Simon,' Jesus said, 'do you love me more than these others do?'

'Yes, Lord,' Simon answered, 'You know that I love you.'

'Feed my lambs,' Jesus responded.

Further along the beach, Jesus again asked, 'Simon, son of John, do you love me?'

'Yes, Lord, you know that I love you,' Simon Peter replied, wondering if Jesus hadn't heard him the first time.

'Take care of my sheep,' Jesus answered.

Even further along the beach, Jesus yet again asked, 'Simon, son of John, do you love me?' Peter was hurt because Jesus asked him the third time, 'Do you love me?' He answered, 'Lord, you know all things; you know that I love you.'

Jesus said, 'Feed my sheep. Truthfully I tell you, when you were younger you were free to choose how to dress and where to go, but when you are older you will stretch out your hands and someone else will dress you, and they will take you where you do not want to go.' Jesus said this because he knew that when Peter died, his death would glorify God.

Then Jesus said to him, 'Follow me!'

RETOLD FROM JOHN 21:15–19

How long

One night, Nicodemus went to Jesus. He wasn't supposed to! He was a Pharisee, a Jewish leader, and his colleagues were not happy with the things Jesus was teaching. But Nicodemus felt he had to talk with Jesus.

'Sir, we know that God has sent you to teach us. I know that you could not work these miracles unless God were with you,' Nicodemus said.

Jesus replied, 'I tell you for certain that you must be born from above before you can see God's kingdom.'

'What do you mean?' Nicodemus asked. 'How can a grown man ever be born a second time?'

Jesus answered, 'I tell you for certain that before you can get into God's kingdom, you must be born not only by water but by the Spirit. Humans give life to their children, but only God's Spirit can change you into a child of God. Don't be surprised when I say you must be born from above. Only God's Spirit gives new life. The Spirit is like the wind that blows wherever it wants. You can hear the wind but you don't know where it comes from or where it is going.'

Nicodemus was puzzled. 'Explain how this can be,' he said.

'How can you be a religious teacher and not know these things?' Jesus answered. 'I tell you for certain that we know what we are talking about because we have seen it ourselves. But you people don't accept what I say. If you don't believe when I talk about things on earth, how can you possibly believe if I talk about things in heaven?

'Everyone who has faith in the Son of Man will have eternal life. You know that God loved the people of this world so much that he gave his only Son, so that everyone who has faith in him will have eternal life and never really die. God didn't send his Son to blame and punish people; he sent him to save them!

'The light has come into the world, but people who do evil things love the dark more than the light. They prefer to stay in the dark, but everyone who lives by God's truth will come into the light and show others what God is doing.'

RETOLD FROM JOHN 3:1–21

How high

Do you love me? This is a question that we often ask, even if we don't use those words. We look for loving actions, kind words, help and support from friends and family and, as humans, we function better knowing that we are loved. Dr Andrew Curren studies the brain. Through all the research he has done, costing millions of pounds, he has discovered and can prove scientifically that the human brain works better and people are better able to learn when they know and feel that they are loved.

'Do you love me?' Three times Jesus asked Peter that question. It is understandable that Jesus would do this, after Peter had denied knowing him three times on the night that Jesus was arrested. Wonder and chat together for a moment about how Simon Peter felt, being asked the same question repeatedly, and how Jesus might have felt asking it.

I wonder how you respond to the question Jesus asked Simon Peter. If God asks you, 'Do you love me?' what will your response be?

How do we show God that we love him? Our 'How long' story today challenges us to think about how we know and live out God's love. If we love God, how do we show other people his love? After all, God's love grows when it's shared, so it is a blessing to us, but the blessing grows when we pass it on too.

How deep

In his first letter, John reminds us what it is to be a Christian when he says:

If we believe that Jesus is truly Christ, we are God's children.
Everyone who loves the Father will also love his children. If we
love and obey God, we know that we will love his children. We
show our love for God by obeying his commandments, and
they are not hard to follow.

1 JOHN 5:1–3

I wonder if you find God's commandments easy or difficult to follow.

What do you want to say to God about his question 'Do you love me'? Tell God what you'd like to say. Ask him what you need to ask. Be quiet and listen to what God wants to say to you.

Love tough

Psalm 90:14 says, 'When morning comes, let your love satisfy all our needs.'

Living in God's ways means that we have to 'love tough' and choose to be different. Talk with God about the question 'Do you love me?' and your responses to it today.

✳

Epilogue

I pray that out of his glorious riches he may strengthen you
with power through his Spirit in your inner being, so that
Christ may dwell in your hearts through faith. And I pray
that you, being rooted and established in love, may have
power, together with all the Lord's holy people, to grasp how
wide and long and high and deep is the love of Christ, and to
know this love that surpasses knowledge—that you may be
filled to the measure of all the fullness of God.

EPHESIANS 3:16–19

- Talk together about how these verses help you be a disciple of Jesus.
- What in this book has helped you as you've grown in God's love?
- On the list of what love is and isn't, what have you found most challenging and most helpful?
- Where have you seen God working in and through you as you've shown his love to others?
- What do you want to say to God about these verses from Ephesians 3? Tell him what you'd like to say. Ask him what you need to ask. Be quiet and listen to what God wants to say to you.

☀

Useful resources

Some of the topics in this book may have raised issues of concern for yourself or a child. Here are some ideas of where to get further help or advice, should it be needed.

Bullying

Every school should have an anti-bullying policy. Contact staff for more details.

Help for children

Childline telephone helpline: 0800 1111
www.childline.org.uk

CEOP (Child Exploitation and Online Protection Centre)
www.thinkuknow.co.uk
www.ceop.gov.uk

Help for concerned adults

Kidscape helpline for adults: 0845 1205 204
www.kidscape.org.uk

NSPCC helpline for adults: 0808 800 5000
www.nspcc.org.uk

Side by Side with God in Everyday Life

Helping children to grow with God through all times

Side by Side with God in Everyday Life invites churches and families alike to use a simple retelling of stories from the Bible as the basis for helping children to think more deeply about a wide range of everyday topics.

In total there are 28 easy-to-use story-based sessions, each featuring one of the times and seasons outlined in Ecclesiastes 3:1–8, such as birth, death, planting, uprooting, laughing, mourning, dancing, giving, listening, love, hate, war and peace.

Each session picks out two related Bible stories, one to set the scene and the other to go deeper into the theme. The idea is that these simple retellings can be used to promote open questions, reflection, discussion, further exploration and prayer, and readily act as prompts towards a deeper understanding of what it means to walk side by side with God in everything we do.

ISBN 978 1 84101 855 3   £7.99
Available from your local Christian bookshop or direct from BRF:
www.brfonline.org.uk.

Parenting Children for a Life of Faith

Helping children meet and know God

Rachel Turner

Nurturing children in the Christian faith is a privilege given to all of us whose prime job it is to raise children. God's desire is that our parenting should guide each child to meet and know him, and to live with him every day through to eternity.

Parenting Children for a Life of Faith explores how the home can become the primary place in which children are nurtured into the reality of God's presence and love, equipped to access him themselves and encouraged to grow in a two-way relationship with him that will last a lifetime. The material explores:

- Discipling our children proactively
- Modelling the reality of being in a relationship with God
- Tying together truth and experience
- Connecting children to God's heart
- Implementing a plan

Each chapter includes true stories and questions to help us reflect on our own experience as we journey together with our children.

ISBN 978 1 84101 607 8   £7.99
Available from your local Christian bookshop or direct from BRF:
www.brfonline.org.uk.

Parenting Children for a Life of Purpose

Empowering children to become who they are called to be

Rachel Turner

'Too long we have stood apart as a church and looked at children and teens and said, "We love you, we value you, but we don't need you."'

Our churches have the power to establish a community of purpose that all people participate in. They can be the places where children feel most powerful, most seen, most discipled and most released. We can be the church that God designed. *Parenting Children for a Life of Purpose* is a practical and tested handbook exploring the possibilities for helping children to discover the specific gifts for whatever God is calling them to be, and showing how parents might partner with churches to enable children to discover their true identity and purpose in life and walk alongside them on the journey.

Addressing issues of identity, relationship, purpose, power, love, calling and response, each chapter includes true stories and questions to help us to reflect on our own experiences.

ISBN 978 0 85746 163 6   £7.99
Available from your local Christian bookshop or direct from BRF:
www.brfonline.org.uk.

Enjoyed
this book?

Write a review—we'd love to hear what you think.
Email: reviews@brf.org.uk

Keep up to date—receive details of our new books as they happen.
Sign up for email news and select your interest groups at:
www.brfonline.org.uk/findoutmore/

Follow us on Twitter @brfonline

By post—to receive new title information by post (UK only), complete
the form below and post to: BRF Mailing Lists, 15 The Chambers, Vineyard,
Abingdon, Oxfordshire, OX14 3FE

Your Details
Name _____
Address_____
_____
Town/City _____ Post Code _____
Email_____

Your Interest Groups (*Please tick as appropriate)	
☐ Advent/Lent	☐ Messy Church
☐ Bible Reading & Study	☐ Pastoral
☐ Children's Books	☐ Prayer & Spirituality
☐ Discipleship	☐ Resources for Children's Church
☐ Leadership	☐ Resources for Schools

Support your local bookshop
Ask about their new title information schemes.